HEAVEN
HELP US

(The Holy Spirit
in Your Life)

by W. Carl Ketcherside

A Division of Standard Publishing
Cincinnati, Ohio
40-001

Library of Congress Catalog Card No. 74-77225
ISBN: 0-87239-007-1

Preface

A flood of books dealing with the Holy Spirit has been pouring from the presses. The emptiness of modern man, coupled with a sense of the futility of earthly existence in a nuclear age, has combined to promote a genuine interest in a Power that can transform life and provide hope of human relationship with the ultimate and infinite. As is true in every age of crisis, much of the appeal to the sensational and emotional is provided purely for the enrichment of the authors.

But many good things of lasting value are being said and written. Further, it is time for men to seek a greater understanding of the will of God and to come to a closer walk with Him through the Spirit. In many respects this volume is different from other such books on this theme now on the market. It is not intended to encourage men to think of the Spirit as a gimmick or fad. It is not the result of a current wave of interest, but it was planned many years ago.

The purpose of the book is to stimulate thought and promote a deeper study of the revealed will of God. I believe that God has spoken, and the revelation of what He has said is contained in the Bible. It is not my intention to be judgmental about the personal experiences to which men and women testify, but I hold that experiences must be judged in the light of the Scriptures, and not the reverse.

The Holy Spirit is not the Word of God; He is the divine agent through whom that Word was conveyed to human agents. The Spirit did not simply deliver the Word and then retire from the scene, however. He took up His abode in the hearts of men to strengthen, aid, and comfort them, in the fulfillment of the divine purpose for their lives. Because of this, this book first identifies the Spirit and then details in practical fashion how He helps us harmonize our lives with the divine will.

The final chapter makes use of material originally written for a journal. It appears in this volume to give it wider circulation and to induce a greater impact upon the lives of those who read it. But simply reading about the Spirit will not enable one to achieve the joy that should be the lot of the redeemed. One can starve to death while studying a cookbook. The Spirit must be allowed to motivate, quicken, and stimulate.

If this little volume leads you into a life of sharing with the Father and all the other members of His family—your brothers and sisters; if it brings freedom from fear of the present; and if it strengthens your faith, it will have achieved its goal and God will be praised.

For the most part, Scripture quotations are from *the Revised Standard Version Bible,* copyright 1946, 1952, and © 1971, by the Division of Christian Education, National Council of the Churches of Christ in the U.S.A., and used by permission. The following abbreviations are used when other versions are quoted: KJV, King James Version; TNEB, The New English Bible.

—W. Carl Ketcherside

Contents

1

The Holy Spirit—Who or What?

Many years ago I attended a Bible-school class in a village church in the heart of the Missouri Ozarks. I was in the region on a bass fishing expedition, and, as my custom was, I attended the services on Sunday morning. I sat in the adult class taught by a local farmer who seemed to be quite knowledgeable about the Bible. His occasional quaint comments made the lesson especially interesting for me.

I surmised, from the discussion by members of the class, that the little town was in a dither because of claims being made by a "faith healer" who was holding forth nightly in the rather decrepit tent. Finally, one man asked, "Well, just what is the Holy Spirit, anyhow? I've heard about it all my life and no one has ever rightly told me what it is." The teacher waited, with a slight smile on his face, until the questioner had finished. Then, holding his well-worn Bible slightly aloft, and waving it for emphasis, he replied, "This Book is the Holy Spirit, and all the Holy Spirit there is. When I have it in my overcoat pocket, the Holy Spirit is in my pocket. The Holy Spirit is the Word of God, and that's what this Book is, the Word of God, and the Holy Spirit."

He looked around the class to see if there were any challengers, but found none. Apparently they had too many burdens to bear in farming their rocky land, in trying to wrest a living from their thin soil, to give much attention to the identity of the Spirit. They were content to leave such questions to the teacher whose respect for the Book caused him to read its pages each night in the soft glow cast by his Aladdin lamp. And since no further questions were forthcoming, the teacher sought to clinch his argument by saying, "Jesus himself said, 'It is the spirit that quickeneth; the flesh profiteth nothing: the words that I speak unto you, they are spirit, and they are life'[John 6:63; KJV]. There it is, as plain as the nose on your face."

I could not be satisfied with the quick response to the tremendous question, "What is the Holy Spirit, anyhow?" Somehow, I was convinced that the quotation drawn from the words of Jesus did not furnish an adequate answer. Although I knew little about the Spirit of God, I had a vague uneasiness at the thought that He could be captured, caught up, and confined to pages bound in black leather, stamped in gold, and crammed into an overcoat pocket. After I retired to my tent, I lay awake pondering a question for which my meager knowledge had no solution. Before I dozed off I made a pledge to learn all I could about the functions assigned to the Spirit. Through the years I have learned much, not the least of which is that almost from the time Jesus promised that the Spirit would come, much confusion has existed about His nature and identity.

I recall talking far into the night with a professor of philosophy in a state university. He had been reared by parents devoted to the Word of God, but during his academic career his own faith had been eroded. This left deep furrows in his intellectual life where the rich topsoil of belief had been washed away by the constant rain of skepticism. He flattered himself that he still maintained faith, but as we conversed it became apparent that his faith was in his own righteousness and in "the wisdom of this passing age" upon which he relied.

"What do you think about the Holy Spirit?" I asked. He looked at me for a minute before he replied. "I believe in a holy spirit, I suppose," he said, "but I do not believe in anything called the Holy Spirit." He gave a lengthy dissertation in scholastic jargon. The gist was that men assign different values to the word "holy," meaning only what each man makes it mean.

He finally explained he thought that the Holy Spirit was merely one's own spirit, his inner self, committed to unselfish sharing with others. It was self, devoted to relieving conditions that affected the social structure for evil, consecrated to working with and through nature for the betterment of all. Pinned down, he confessed that he was a humanist, and the expression "Holy Spirit" was merely a catchword, a handle with which to turn off religious discussion. The Holy Spirit no longer had any real relevance for him.

Then there was the wealthy manufacturer who invited me to his palatial home to talk about his idea of God and the created universe. In his voluminous library we sat down to canvass the thinking of each other. He proved to be a mystic and a student of esoteric religions. His idea of the Holy Spirit was that of a nebulous, pervasive influence, which invaded all religion and led men to a higher degree of achievement through art forms and literary productions. He regarded the Bible as inspired, but only as he thought the works of Rembrandt, Titian, or Shakespeare were inspired. The Holy Spirit was the rarefied atmosphere breathed by the gifted, the composite influence derived from heredity, training, and fellowship with others. He thought the tendency was ever upward and onward. He fully expected that this certain but subtle influence would so affect the world that someday men would become more godlike, and sorrow and suffering would be conquered and pass away. The world would be saved by its art and literature.

My affluent friend regaled me with various quotations from eminent philosophers, but the widely divergent views caused me to explore my favorite field, history, to see if the same kind of confusion existed in earlier times among those who professed to be believers in Christ. I was not too greatly surprised to find that such was the case. I should like to share with you a few highlights of this research.

If you are inclined to think that the contemporary problems of the Christian world are multitudinous, you need only to read the account of conditions in the first four centuries to realize that by comparison we are in relatively calm waters. That "the Way" has survived at all is a testimony to God's providential care and concern. Whereas many of our debates are about peripheral matters, those of which we speak struck at the very nature of the Godhead. The real questions were related to the identity of Jesus, but these resolved into disputes about the Holy Spirit as well. Here are some of the reasons for controversies that divided and fragmented the primitive believers:

First, the gospel was taken to the Jews, and the original community of saints was composed of Jews and proselytes. To many Jews it appeared, and still does, that disciples of Jesus were affirming the existence of three deities, and since they measured all teaching by the revelation of God in the *Torah* and *Hafterah*, the Law and the Prophets, they had to rationalize the subordination of the Son and the Holy Spirit.

The problem was intensified with the destruction of Jerusalem in 70 A.D., and the consequent scattering of the Jewish community of believers. Gradually the members who were dispersed drifted into a denial of the divinity of Jesus. They regarded only the Gospel according to Matthew as valid, and they considered Paul an apostate. Since they proscribed all of his epistles, they could not use them as source materials with reference to the Spirit. Eventually they came to regard Jesus as a creation of God and the Spirit as a creation of Jesus. The Spirit thus became a son of Jesus as Jesus was a son of God, which is the equivalent of saying that the Spirit was God's grandson.

Second, the term for "spirit" originally meant "breath" or "wind." This is true in Hebrew, Greek, Latin, and even in Anglo-Saxon. In Hebrew the original is *ruach*, in Greek *pneuma*, in Latin *spiritus*, and in English, *ghost*. In every instance the original means "blow" or "breath." For this reason, many believers in the early centuries of the faith came to think of the Spirit as merely an impersonal force,

11

with no more consciousness than the wind or breath. Certain expressions in the divine revelation seemed to lend force to their deduction. John records an incident after the resurrection when Jesus suddenly stood among the disciples and invoked peace upon them. "And when he had said this, he breathed on them, and said to them, Receive the Holy Spirit" (John 20:22). The conclusion was that the Spirit was merely the breath of God.

When the apostles were present on the Day of Pentecost, awaiting the overwhelming of the Spirit as promised, "suddenly a sound came from heaven like the rush of a mighty wind, and it filled all the house where they were sitting" (Acts 2:2). No wind filled the house. The sound was like the noise of a gale, and since "they were all filled with the Holy Spirit," it was an easy matter to think of wind and Spirit as interchangeable.

The early disciples, however, like many of the cultists in our own day, overlooked certain facts about language. They were trapped into trying to fit every use of the word for Spirit into their own little traditional cubicles. Language is like the persons who employ it for communication. It is not static. It is constantly growing and changing. It tends always to expand and become broader in scope. One can no more force acquired usage into primitive root meanings than he can, in his maturity, force his body into the trousers he wore to kindergarten.

Thus the versatile Greeks extended the word *pneuma* beyond its basic meaning of a movement of air, or the breath of the nostrils, to the vital principle by which the body is animated. From that they went on, through a logical sequence, to the rational spirit, the power by which a human being thinks, feels, wills, and decides. Eventually, the spirit in man came to be recognized as that part of man which is rational, giving him the power to perceive and grasp divine things, so that the Spirit of God can exert an influence upon him.

At this point I suggest that the serious student can avail himself of what is commonly referred to in our day as Thayer's *Greek-English Lexicon of the New Testament*. The foregoing definition was adapted from it. Actually, this helpful volume was not produced by Joseph Thayer, but by C. L. Willibald Grimm, an Austrian who expanded and improved upon a work by C. G. Wilke. Thayer translated it into English and made some revision. This is mentioned because Dr. Grimm, in his *Prospectus*, announced that one of his purposes was "to exhibit the historical growth of a word's significance and accordingly in selecting vouchers for New Testament usage to show at what time and in what class of writers a given word became current."[1]

My goal is not to produce a volume for advanced scholars. It is to share insights with those who love the Lord and the written Word, whose opportunity for research is limited both by lack of time and the need for making a living. I have written this because of the imposition of certain cultists who disturb the minds of the unlearned by insisting that, since the root meaning of "spirit" is wind or breath, when a

---

[1] C. L. Willibald Grimm, *Clavis Novi Testamenti Philologica* (*Prospectus*) (Leipzig: Arnoldische Buchhandlung, 1862).

man ceases to breathe the spirit ceases to exist. This conclusion I deem to be neither Scriptural nor sensible.

Again, I am indebted to the lexicographer mentioned above for pointing out Martin Luther's statement that the pneuma is "the highest and noblest part of man, which qualifies him to lay hold of the incomprehensible, invisible, eternal things; in short, it is the house where Faith and God's Word are at home."[2]

A third and fruitful source of conflict and confusion about the Spirit has been the rise of cult leaders who projected false opinions, causing millions to be misled and to follow in their wake. Some of these were sincere but self-deceived, while others were simply deceivers motivated by their own ambition. It was not always easy to distinguish the class in which each one belonged, but the damage done by the schismatic teaching was generally the same.

It is axiomatic that like causes produce like results. This is as true in the religious realm as in any other. In times of ferment and social upheaval, when "the hearts of men fail them for fear," an element of mysticism takes over, and out of this is spawned a kind of fanaticism, which grasps at strange and bizarre doctrines for a ray of hope. An outstanding example of this occurred about the middle of the second century, perhaps in the decade following A.D. 160. In Phrygia, the worship of the goddess Cybele was predominant. This female deity was re-

---

[2]Joseph Henry Thayer, *A Greek-English Lexicon of the New Testament* (New York: Harper and Brothers, 1889), p. 520.

garded as the earth-mother and the source of all life. Her priests, called Corybantes, led in the worship, which was frenzied and orgiastic, generally conducted in sylvan glades or in the depths of dark forests.

One of these priests, Montanus, became a convert to Christianity. He sought to inject into Christianity the same excitability and emotional excess that had accompanied his pagan ministrations. He imagined and announced that he was the Paraclete, the "other Comforter" whom Jesus had promised to send to earth upon His return to glory. Montanus was subject to raptures during which, according to his testimony, the divine took over in his life, and used his tongue to utter enigmatic and mystic expressions, which were interpreted as messages of Heaven to the saints.

Montanus declared that the return of Christ was imminent and would occur during the lifetime of those present. His coming would usher in a thousand years' reign, a millennium in which the Lord would personally rule over the earth and straighten out the tangled state into which sin had plunged the universe. In preparation for this, Montanus called upon the believers to exercise rigid discipline over themselves and to redouble their efforts to convert mankind. Frequent fasts were imposed; celibacy was recommended; and second marriages were unconditionally forbidden. Mortification of the body was enjoined, and the unkempt appearance with tattered garments was encouraged as a sign of humility and self-denial in preparation for the end of the existing order.

Two women, Priscilla and Maximilla, also visionaries, were proclaimed to be prophetesses. They traveled with Montanus as "companions of the Paraclete." They also were preoccupied with the thought of the last days. Epiphanius has preserved a statement of Maximilla to the effect that, "After me there will not again be a prophetess, but the end will come." Priscilla claimed to have seen the Lord himself. She testified that He appeared in the form of a woman attired in shining garb, to inform her that the New Jerusalem would soon descend from Heaven and settle upon the earth at Pepuza, in Asia Minor.

I beg the kind indulgence of my readers for inserting here what may appear to be a too lengthy statement from the book, *The Early Church*, written by David Duff, an eminent professor of church history in Edinburgh, Scotland. The following quotation points up those conditions which seem to bring to the forefront mere human beings who imagine that they are either the Holy Spirit, or His authorized spokesmen:

"Montanism had something of the character of a revival. It was the first reaction, while the Church was still young, against a widespread lukewarmness and worldliness, and especially against the slothful, if not the scoffing spirit of the multitude of believers who no longer cherished the lively expectation of the *parousia* of Christ, which had been so general in the first days, but said, 'The Lord delayeth His coming,' forgetting that one day with the Lord is as a thousand years, and a thousand years as one day. It is not wonderful that, in these circumstances, many should be dissatisfied with themselves, dissatisfied with the Church, dissatisfied with the episcopal rulers, who were now consolidating their power. But here were enthusiasts, who sought not only to recall the lost ideal, but, in view of the approaching end, and under the inspiration of the Paraclete, to make Christianity holier and purer than in the days of the apostles. Their ecstasies, their zeal, their rigorism, and even their spiritual pride, were fitted to gain them adherents far and wide, and possibly the fear of those Gnostic speculations by which the objective truths of Christianity were subverted had a powerful influence with not a few, and induced them to embrace or favor a system in which the objectivity of Christianity, and particularly the doctrine of the *parousia*, was made to absorb the thought and energy of the individual."[3]

The persistent student of church history will soon become aware that at intervals there is a recurrence of almost universal concern with the Holy Spirit and His activity on the contemporary scene. When the religious structures become solidified and those who maintain them become adamant, when worldliness and apathy rule the lives of the membership, those whose deep emotional needs are not being met seek a closer walk with God, and a visible manifestation of the presence of the Spirit. It is easier to walk by sight in a world of fear and trepidation than to walk by faith.

In every such period men like Montanus arise, and if they do not, as he did, claim to be the Holy Spirit personified, they do profess to be His Vicars. They produce prophecies that the uninitiated are

---

[3]David Duff, M.A., D.D., LL.D., *The Early Church* (Edinburgh: T. and T. Clark, 1891), p. 206.

expected to receive unquestioningly, under threat of damnation for refusal. Repeatedly there has been a reaffirmation that the last days are at hand. When the world becomes so complex and confused that men can find no solution in social experiments and political expediencies, they turn toward God.

As it is with so many other things in human life, there are both good and bad features involved in such a cyclical process. It is good that men are brought to a realization of the need of God's influence in human affairs, and good that the power and impact of the Holy Spirit are once more affirmed. It is regrettable that the daily and constant concern of God for mankind is so soon forgotten after the excitement and agitation have died away. It is also a tragedy that many historians, aware of the predictions, which never come to pass, conclude that the whole Christian fabric has been woven from the overheated imaginations of men without real basis in fact. Nothing could be farther from the truth. Because Jesus has not returned at the time appointed by men does not mean that He will not return at the time appointed by the Father.

It will be helpful, I think, to study carefully the words of a German historian and analyst, K. R. Hagenbach, who in about 1850 wrote the following:

> "Has not at all times a rigid way of life, especially when it arms itself with a prophetic, enthusiastic speech, and turns itself against the existing order of things, produced a mighty impression on the multitude? To observe with all wisdom and patience the quiet course of God in history, and to follow its traces even where the natural eye per-

ceives only a natural succession of events, belongs only to the man who has been exercised and trained in spiritual things. The mass loves the astounding, the thoroughgoing, the uncompromising; and hence the extraordinary outpourings, the improvised prophecies, of a heated and extravagant imagination, supported by an energetic will, have ever imposed more on the rude mind than the harmonious exhibition of a calm and simple piety. Montanism is not an isolated phenomenon. Distrust of science, contempt for heathen literature, hostility to art and culture, a bold disregard of established social relations and forms, a rough exterior, a constant prominence given to repentance, coupled with predictions of fearful judgments—such marks the Montanists have in common not only with the different sects of the Middle Ages, and the Anabaptists of the age of the Reformation, but more or less, with the Puritans of England and the Camisards of France, and the many 'awakened' (so-called) of more recent and most recent times."[4]

The validity of the thesis of Hagenbach is established by the fact that it might have been written within our own generation without changing a word or sentence. It would be surprisingly easy to show the various periods to which he alludes that men have been carried away on a wave of enthusiasm, repetitious of other such occasions produced by the state of the world in previous times. This procedure, however, would be only incidental to our real purpose at present and we must postpone it until a more propitious season.

---

[4]K. R. Hagenbach, *Vorless u. Wesen u Gesch* (Leipzig, 1851).

Let me then summarize what I have said. I have asserted that the present confusion about the Holy Spirit is not a unique phenomenon. Much misunderstanding about the nature, essence, and work of the Spirit has characterized every age. I have sought to show that some of the perplexity has originated in an ignorance of the Godhead, and the conjecture that an admission of the personality of the Spirit would demand an assumption that there existed a plurality of Gods.

Again, I have shown that uncertainty has arisen because of the etymology of *spirit*, and the failure to recognize that words, as do trees, grow from roots, and that such growth necessitates change. One can no more develop a language by insisting that root meanings must remain static than he can produce fruit by cutting off every shoot that springs above the surface of the soil from the roots below.

I have also given proof that professed teachers have deceived the multitudes through the centuries, either by alleging that they were the Spirit incarnated, or by claiming to be special functionaries of the Spirit, with new and fanciful revelations that appealed to the credulous.

It is now time to turn from this avenue of approach to study and analyze the teachings of the Scriptures with reference to the identity of the Holy Spirit. As we do this it will be necessary to avoid the dogmatic and authoritarian attitude. In a spirit of sharing let us turn to a continued investigation of the nature of the profound relationship between the Holy Spirit and the human spirit. Surely no greater theme than this can challenge the intellect.

2

Is the Spirit the Word?

Is the Holy Spirit the Word of God? Is the Spirit a pervasive influence of righteousness, or the spirit of man consecrated to a service to humanity, simply because "holy is as holy does"? The only source from which to obtain an answer to these questions is the revelation of God. Revelation, from the Greek *apokalupsis*, means laying bare, making naked, or uncovering. It relates to God's unveiling that which otherwise must remain a mystery to man.

There is a sphere beyond the ability of man's intellect to probe and penetrate. Being finite, man is circumscribed in the range of knowledge to what he can apprehend by his senses and to what he can deduct by rational thought processes. By memory he can recall the past, and by imagination he can project himself into the realm of fantasy, but he cannot know divine thought without divine revelation.

One who postulates that man is the creation of an intelligent Being will accept as a corollary that such a Creator will communicate to His creation. Thus, the fact of revelation is substantiated by the nature of God and man, since only God can supply the need of man for that knowledge which is beyond his grasp.

The apostle Paul declares that what could not be ascertained by the eye, or learned by hearing or rational perception, has been revealed to man by the

Spirit. He affirms that the Holy Spirit sustains the same relationship to the mind of God that the human spirit does to the human mind and that, therefore, the Holy Spirit alone is able to reveal the thoughts of God.

Revelation is the uncovering for man by the Holy Spirit of what man cannot discover for himself. There is a difference between the undiscovered and the undiscoverable. The first is capable of being found out by additional research, while the last is beyond man's power to fathom without divine assistance. God never reveals to man what he can learn by his own study or be taught by another, for to do this would be to circumvent the very rational powers He gave to man. These are the means by which man is distinguished from the rest of the animal kingdom and exhibits the image of God.

The Holy Spirit is a subject for and of revelation. We can grasp the nature and identity of the Spirit only from a study of the Word of God. We cannot do research into the existence of the Spirit by means of our sensory apparatus, nor by use of our perceptive powers. In clarifying for us the identity of the Spirit, God's revelation will also disabuse our minds of false concepts and free us from mistaken ideas.

To begin with, it seems obvious to me that the Spirit is not the Word of God. These two bear a close relationship to one another and work together in a harmonious way, but they are not identical in any sense. The Word of God has been manifested in three forms: the living Word, the oral word, and the written word. In none of these forms is the Word to be confounded with the Spirit.

The Greek term for the living Word is *Logos*. This was the term for both reason and word. If we think of these in a purely contemporary sense, as we now employ them, we will not do justice to them, nor assign to them the values that they exhibit when employed in the Scriptures. We generally think of reason simply as an intellectual process, and of a word as a mere symbol of thought. But the ancient philosophers regarded both in a much more profound light. A recognition of this will enable us to understand their use in God's revelation. Reason was creative. The origin and order of the cosmos were attributable to it. Before the material universe existed, reason was. It gave form and meaning to all else. It was the only primal reality, the first cause. As everything existed in an idealistic concept before it was translated into being, reason was the womb out of which all else was delivered. The sculptor could summon the form of reason from marble and give it a body as he did other qualities and attributes of deity, and when he did the statue was worshiped as a god.

In the same way the wise-men of old regarded words. Words were not carelessly used as they often are now, because they were looked upon as possessing life. Indeed, they were thought of as having souls and bodies. The soul was the thought, the vital imagery given birth in the mind, while the sounds or written characters constituted the body in which it was encased. Words could be mutilated by ridicule and distortion of the thought, or they could be murdered by destruction of their message.

Various forms of illustration were devised to portray the power of words to effect change in the universe. They were as arrows shot forth from an unseen bow, and sometimes they were poison bringing death to those who received them into their hearts. Sometimes they were aflame, setting on fire the passions of men and consuming them. They were also looked upon as birds winging their way from a mental dovecote and carrying messages to distant realms. Certainly they were not "dead letters" or dry material, although they might be referred to as chaff.

Recognition of these things will help us appreciate more fully the testimony of the apostle John, who wrote to counter the inroads of Gnosticism, a dangerous philosophy that threatened the existence of "the Way" in the Greek world. Our present purpose will not be served by lengthy explanation of this pernicious doctrine, but prominent among its tenets was advocacy of the idea that all matter is inherently evil, and God could not involve himself directly with man in the flesh. The Gnostics, who took their name from gnosis (wisdom), had much to say about the Logos as the impersonal creative wisdom out of which the world was conceived.

John begins his testimony of Jesus as the Messiah and Son of God by the affirmation, "In the beginning was the [Logos], and the [Logos] was with God, and the [Logos] was God. The same was in the beginning with God. All things were made by him; and without him was not any thing made that was made" (John 1:1-3; KJV). The Logos is here portrayed as personal, and not impersonal. He was Creator and not created. When the beginning occurred He was already existent. Place the beginning where you will, but He was already there.

The Logos was with God, so there existed God and the Logos. But the Logos was God. He was Deity. He was not one who existed with God as of a different nature and character. He existed not from the beginning, but in the beginning, uncreated and creating, so the Logos was God.

John then makes an interesting commentary about the Logos' relationship to man. "In him was life; and the life was the light of men. And the light shineth in darkness; and the darkness comprehended it not" (vv. 4, 5; KJV). The expression, "in him was life," does not mean merely that He was alive. Such a statement would have been unnecessary. The Logos was the repository of life. He was the origin of all life as we know and experience it, but He was not the creator of life. Life is uncreated and eternal. In a sense God is life, for just as there was never a time when God was not, so there was never a time when life was not. Of course, like Paul, I speak after the manner of men because of the infirmity of the flesh. The expression "a time" as used here is awkward because Deity is not subject to time or space.

The light that was in the beginning in the Logos is the light of men. Life, then, is more than existence. It is illumination. It is a sharing of the divine with the human, a bestowal of the divine energy, the creative urge upon man as a rational being made in the image of God and the Logos. It is the life that is the light, and man by his very nature—his human nature—is instinctively within the range of that light.

Sin brought a pall of darkness upon the universe. It was not created to be in darkness, but in light. Sin changed "the course of this world" and surrendered it to the dominion of the prince of the power of the air, under whose reign the children of disobedience produce "the unfruitful works of darkness." Still, the life, which is the light, continues to bring its impact upon the darkness, and the darkness is not able to overcome it. It cannot engulf or swallow up the light. Just as light is superior to darkness, so life is superior to death. When one moves in, the other must surrender its tenancy.

We come now to the capsheaf of John's witness. "And the [Logos] was made flesh, and dwelt among us . . . full of grace and truth" (v. 14; KJV). This statement bewildered the Greek world and challenged its thinking as nothing did. Even in our own day many persons find it extremely difficult to accept. The word for "dwelt" in the original means tent or tabernacle. What John is saying is that the Logos was made flesh and brought His own tent (body) with Him. He came to share our nomadic life as strangers and pilgrims on the earth.

The Holy Spirit is not the living Word. That Word became incarnate as the Son of God, and when the sonship was publicly recognized, the Spirit descended upon Him as a divine attestation of His relationship. It all happened when Jesus presented himself to John the baptizer to be baptized in the Jordan River. Here is the account of what happened: "The next day John seeth Jesus coming unto him, and saith, Behold the Lamb of God, which taketh away the sin of the world. This is he of whom I said, After me cometh a man which is preferred before me: for he was before me. And I knew him not: but that he should be made manifest to Israel, therefore am I come baptizing with water. And John bare record, saying, I saw the Spirit descending from heaven like a dove, and it abode upon him. And I knew him not: but he that sent me to baptize with water, the same said unto me, Upon whom thou shalt see the Spirit descending, and remaining on him, the same is he which baptizeth with the Holy Ghost. And I saw, and bare record that this is the Son of God" (John 1:29-34; KJV).

We cannot determine whether or not John was personally acquainted with Jesus before He came to be baptized. It is possible that the expression, "I knew him not" referred to recognition as the Messiah who should be presented to Israel. John had instructions to prepare the hearts of the Jews by giving them knowledge of salvation through the remission of their sins. He was informed that when he would see the Spirit of God descend in the bodily form of a dove and remain upon the One whom he was baptizing, he would know that He was the Son of God.

At the beginning of Jesus' personal ministry there was a distinction between the Spirit and the Son. The two are never confused in the New Covenant Scriptures. In a disputed passage (1 John 5:7) occurs the statement, "For there are three that bear record in heaven, the Father, the Word, and the Holy Ghost: and these three are one" (KJV). Even though this does not appear in the oldest and best manuscripts, and may be in interpolation from the marginal notes of an early translator or transcriber, its message is true. There are three, and yet they are one.

Just as the Holy Spirit is not the living Word, so the Spirit is not the oral word as delivered by the apostles and prophets. In a memorable section of his first letter to the Corinthians, Paul discusses his initial approach to their city. It had given its very name to licentiousness and vice of the lowest degree. Here lust was worshiped as homage to the goddess of love, and deviant sex was regarded as a means of expressing religion. In this setting Paul came with a message of cleansing, sanctification, and justification in the name of the Lord Jesus, and by the Spirit of God (6:11).

When the apostle arrived in the city, which prided itself upon the very philosophy that had resulted in an urban sprawl of immorality, he refused to engage in the kind of rhetoric so popular in the Greek world. He specifically affirmed, "When I came to you to present the evidence for the secret of God, which it was my purpose to declare, I rejected the eloquent vocabulary associated with philosophy" (paraphrase of 1 Corinthians 2:1).

The difference between the philosophers and the apostle is simply stated. The philosophers took what was plain and left it a mystery; the apostle took what was a mystery and made it plain. To Paul, the string that unraveled the secret of the ages was the cross. Thus, he declared, "I determined not to know any thing among you, save Jesus Christ, and him crucified" (1 Corinthians 2:2).

Having committed himself to this course, Paul freely admitted that he personally felt a sense of his own weakness, accompanied by dread and great trembling. This does not mean that he was ready to "press the panic button," nor does it imply that he was frightened by what might happen to him personally. He was deeply concerned about the reception of his testimony. Accordingly, he declared that his language and message were not set forth in plausible words of wisdom.

It is a common trick of hucksters to conceal inferior and unacceptable fruit in the bottom of a container and the better fruit on top. In much the same way the philosophers were masters in the art of enticement through carefully planned usage of vocabulary. The apostle scorned the employment of such methods. He wrote: "For we are not, like so many, peddlers of God's word; but as men of sincerity, as commissioned by God, in the sight of God we speak in Christ" (2 Corinthians 2:17). He did not put the cross in the bottom of the basket to be discovered later by those who were attracted to Jesus. Christ's death on the cross was placed on top for everyone to see. That death, not a higher degree of moral conduct, made redemption a fact. The speech and message were, therefore, in demonstration of the Spirit and power, in order that the faith of those who heard would not rest in human philosophy, the wisdom of men, but in the power of God. Men were to be captured for Christ, not by being blindfolded or hoodwinked by persuasive eloquence, but by the influence of the Spirit and the dynamic of the thing proclaimed. The content of the message, not the wrapper in which it was packed, was to transform profligate Corinth.

A realization of this will preclude a common error created by the King James Version, which renders 1 Corinthians 1:21, "For after that in the wisdom of God the world by wisdom knew not God, it pleased God by the foolishness of preaching to save them that believe." Many students conclude that this merely refers to the act of preaching. But nothing in the mere act of proclaiming will save anyone.

The original word for "preaching" is *kerygma*, which refers to the thing proclaimed, the message announced. The thesis of the apostle is that the Jews were waiting for a demonstration of power to save them as their fathers were rescued from enslavement in Egypt. Meanwhile, the Greeks were seeking to transcend the human experience by the sheer attainment of logic.

God allowed man to get to the point where he realized the futility and powerlessness of human rationality to effect a change. It was not until human wisdom had exhausted its possibilities and man had sunk to the depths of degradation that God intervened. Paul described what happened: God waited until the divine wisdom dictated that man had sufficiently demonstrated that human wisdom was incapable of discovering the divine, and at that time it pleased Him by the proclamation of a historical event, which seemed foolish, to save them that believe.

The event was the death of Christ. The thing preached was the crucifixion. To the Jew the cross was a scandal; to the Greek it was simply absurd. It was foolishness. Thus, those who were saved by trusting in the cross manifested a faith that was not grounded in the wisdom of men, but in the power of God.

In 1 Corinthians 2:6, Paul speaks of "the wisdom of this world," that is, of this passing age. In the following verse he contrasts it with the wisdom of God, which is not transitory but was ordained before the world, that is, decreed before the ages. While man was seeking to penetrate the veil of the future, God was biding His time, waiting in infinite patience for the right moment to draw aside the veil of His own secret. Finally, what man could not ascertain by visual or audible testimony, and what he could not deduce by his rational processes was revealed by the Spirit. The Spirit sustains the same relationship to God as the human spirit does to man. Only the inner man is aware of the thoughts, intents, and purposes of the man. Likewise, no one outside knows or comprehends the thoughts of the Infinite except the Spirit of God.

It is important for us to remember that thought cannot be conveyed from one mind to another without a medium of communication. Thought occurs as imagery in the mind, but that imagery cannot be projected without one's employing mutually accepted symbols. With the use of such symbols the imagery is reproduced in the receptive mind.

The highest form of communication known to rational beings is that of speech. It is a God-given faculty, for God not only created the organs of speech, but apparently taught man the use of them. No man has ever spoken who was not first spoken to, and it is evident that man did not invent or develop speech. God spoke to man, and man learned to speak.

Speech makes use of language, and all language

was at first oral. The very word is from *lingua*, tongue. When God was ready to unravel the secret of the ages, the revelation was given by the Spirit, as the divine agent. And the Spirit, in conformity with God's recognition of man as a rational being, capable of receiving and understanding messages conveyed in language, made use of words to unveil the mystery.

Paul wrote that he spoke the things God freely revealed to us, not in words taught by human philosophers, but as revealed by the Holy Spirit, who enables us to interpret spiritual truths in spiritual language (v. 13).

We need to be careful in our approach to this statement. It does not mean that the Spirit invented a new or sacred vocabulary, and used it as a vehicle to transmit the divine message. To have done this would have defeated the purpose of God, for it would not have been a revelation at all. What is meant is simply that the words used by men were adopted and adapted to communicate or transmit divine thought. This is in harmony with the practice and purpose of God.

When God was ready to allow the Living Word to be made flesh, He did not create a new type of body, just as when the written Word was recorded it did not require a new body of type. The Word became flesh by being conceived in a human womb, and delivered by the same birth process as every human being. Jesus stripped himself in order to assume the guise of a slave in that He became like men and was born a human being. And the spoken word came in the linguistic form of everyday existence.

The difference in the body of Christ and the bodies of other men was not in composition but in the spirit within. The difference in the words of revelation and those of ordinary communication is that the Spirit infused the first. It would appear that anyone could see that the Spirit was not identical with the words of the apostles. There is a difference between a teacher and the words he employs, and Paul is quite plain in saying, "We speak these things in the words the Holy Spirit teaches" (v. 13).

Why do some men eagerly seek to identify the Spirit with the spoken word? It is possible that they want to be able to control, to manage, and manipulate the Spirit. Men can exercise control of words and make them their servants. If the Holy Spirit can be equated with the spoken word, then the Spirit comes under the management of men. The Spirit will be dependent upon the will and volition of men.

What has been said about the oral message is also true of the message committed to writing. There is no difference. What the apostles taught while they were present with the brethren is the same thing they wrote when they were absent from them. Consider such expressions as the following: "Do you not remember that when I was still with you I told you this? . . . For even when we were with you, we gave you this command" (2 Thessalonians 2:5; 3:10). For this reason the admonition could be given, "So then, brethren, stand firm and hold to the traditions which you were taught by us, either by word of mouth or by letter" (2:15).

The Holy Spirit never was the Word of God and is not now bound into a volume. The Spirit cannot be set in type, or placed on tape. The Spirit cannot be imprinted on a press or purchased at a bookstore. The written Word is the effective instrument, or word of the Spirit. "And take the helmet of salvation, and the sword of the Spirit, which is the word of God" (Ephesians 6:17; KJV).

Our responsibility is to study the revealed Word, made available to us through the grace of God and by the Holy Spirit. No one can be true to his Christian commitment who derogates either the work of the Spirit or the need for knowledge of the Word. It is not a matter of the Spirit or the Word, but rather of the Spirit and the Word. One can never get a sufficient measure of the Spirit that he no longer needs the Word, nor can he attain to such a degree of knowledge that he no longer needs the Spirit.

It is true that the more one thinks about and appreciates the work of the Spirit, the more ardent will become his desire to acquaint himself with the words of the Spirit. The greater one's knowledge of the Word becomes, the more fervently will he seek the glorious companionship of the Spirit. It is a strangely warped view of God's program for our spiritual growth when one concludes that, because of his acquaintance with the Spirit, he can ignore further research into the Word that the Spirit delivered as God's will for mankind.

3

What Does the Spirit Do?

The sincere follower of Jesus seeks to shape his career on earth by the words and deeds of the Lord. Surrender of the life to Jesus means more than one's merely trying to do better according to a new code of rules and regulations. It is not the turning over of a new leaf, but one's turning up with a new life. I am reluctant to say that it means adoption of a new life style, for this implies that one may choose to live by other styles. If Jesus is rejected, what is chosen is not life at all, but death. "He that hath the Son hath life; and he that hath not the Son of God hath not life" (1 John 5:12; KJV). What is set before man is not a variety of life styles from which to make a selection. God is not operating on a glorified cafeteria basis. He has said, "See, I have set before thee this day life and good, and death and evil" (Deuteronomy 30:15; KJV). To walk in the steps of Jesus means more than merely to change direction, although that is obviously involved. When one is crucified to the world and the world is crucified to him, he no longer lives to the world. He is dead. If he is to exist, another must live in him, seeing through his eyes, speaking with his tongue, and thinking through his brain.

Such a representative of the new humanity does not question whether the life of Jesus will be practical or expedient, or whether it will "pay off." The initial decision takes care of all of that. When he ascertains the manner in which Jesus regarded a question and the language Jesus used, he simply speaks of it in that manner.

A good example of this is found in the attitude toward the identity of the Holy Spirit. The follower of Jesus regards the Spirit as did Jesus. When the Christian speaks of the Spirit he does so in the language Jesus employed. The vocabulary of Jesus becomes his vocabulary. He not only speaks where the Bible speaks, but he speaks as the Bible speaks. When he speaks about the Spirit he means the same thing Jesus meant when speaking of the Spirit.

Even the most casual reader will at once see that Jesus regarded the Spirit as a person. It would be impossible in the limited compass of this chapter to explore fully every reference made by Jesus to the Spirit. Fortunately, that will not be necessary for our purpose. We may limit our study to one discourse delivered in the upper room in Jerusalem, just before Jesus' betrayal and crucifixion. The record of this address is found in John 13—16.

John prefaces the discourse with the statement that Jesus knew His hour had come to depart from this world to the Father. Having loved His own who were in the world, He loved them to the end. The experience was traumatic for both Jesus and the disciples, as He who prepared to depart from the world must prepare the others to remain in the world. The announcement of His impending exodus was made firmly, but gently. "Little children, yet a little while I am with you. You will seek me; and as I said to the Jews so now I say to you, 'Where I am going you cannot come' " (John 13:33).

This immediately aroused questions, and as usual, Peter put them into words: "Lord, where are you going?" The answer was not direct or definitive. Instead, it cut to the real heart of the matter, that of continued intimate association. Jesus replied, " 'Where I am going you cannot follow me now; but you shall follow me afterward.' " This did not satisfy Peter, who quickly interjected, "Lord, why cannot I follow you now? I will lay down my life for you." Jesus said that before the cock would crow for the morning watch, Peter would deny Him three times. Instead of Peter's laying down his life for Jesus, he would lay down Jesus for his life.

Jesus' announcement of His departure brought consternation to the troubled hearts of His followers, and He sought to allay their fears. He assured them that in spite of the fact they would not be able to see Him as before, their relationship would not be dissolved. There would be no loss of *power*. " 'He who believes in me will also do the works that I do; and greater works than these will he do, because I go to the Father' " (14:12). There would be no loss of *communication*. " 'Whatever you ask in my name, I will do it, that the Father may be glorified in the Son' " (v. 13). There would be no loss of *companionship*. " 'I will not leave you desolate; I will come to you' " (v. 18).

The word rendered "desolate" is the Greek word *orphanos*. Literally it means one who is bereft of a father or parents. The word is translated "fatherless" in James 1:27. When Jesus announced His imminent departure, He addressed the disciples as "little children." This indicates that He regarded them not only

37

as a father would his offspring, but as young children, immature and relatively helpless. He informs them that they will not be abandoned or cast adrift as orphans, but He will come to them.

A study of the context will show that Jesus was going to request the Father to send another Helper or Comforter, and that this Helper would be so like Him that He could be considered as His other self. The association would be so remarkably intimate that it could be regarded as the Father and Son dwelling in them. " 'If a man loves me, he will keep my word, and my Father will love him, and we will come to him and make our home with him' " (v. 23).

The original word Jesus used for this new Companion was *Parakletos*. It is difficult to find an English term to do justice to this Greek word, and translators differ in the terms they select for translation. The word means, "one who stands beside another to render assistance in time of need." Translators of the *King James Version* selected the word "Comforter" to designate the work of the Spirit, and "Advocate" to designate the work of Jesus (1 John 2:1)—the only other time the original occurs. Only John employs the word in the Scriptures.

The word "Comforter" may be somewhat misleading in this age because of our "watering down" of the meaning of comfort. Once the word had to do with strength and defense in time of attack, as the word "fort" indicates. A fortress was a bulwark against death and the destruction of all that one held dear. The word "comfort" is from the Latin *comfortare*, to make strong. So a comforter was one who brought power to hold out against attacking forces. In the days of King James I the word was a good one to employ for "*Paraclete*."

The Revised Standard Version uses "Counselor," and this reflects much the same idea as "Advocate." The Greeks used *parakletos* to describe an attorney who appeared beside one in court to advise and defend. This idea is still found in such words as judge-advocate and counselor-at-law. *The New English Bible* employs the word "Advocate," while *Today's English Version* uses "Helper."

That Jesus regarded the Spirit as a divine person seems apparent from His language when He said, "I will pray the Father, and he shall give you another [Helper], that he may abide with you for ever" (John 14:16; KJV). The Greek had two words for "another": *heteros*, which means "another of a different kind"; and *allos*, which means "another of the same kind." The latter is used here. The Spirit was to be another Helper, like Jesus. Just as God sent Jesus as a Helper, He would now send the Spirit in the same role. True, Jesus brought His own tent with Him; that is, He came in a body. The Spirit, on the other hand, did not come in His own body, for He was to dwell in the bodies of believers. "He dwelleth with you, and shall be in you" (v. 17).

So personal would the relationship with the Spirit become that it would compensate for the absence of Jesus. The Spirit would be with the disciples forever, literally, through the age in which Jesus is absent. The saints of God are never to be desolate or orphaned by the absence of Jesus. The other Helper, who succeeded Jesus on the earth, will be succeeded only by the return of Jesus.

No one who seriously studies the language of the Lord can fail to note the use of the masculine pronoun in the references to the Spirit. This is especially singular when we remember that *pneuma* is the word for spirit, and in its original usage meant wind, breath, and sometimes air. For this reason it is generally represented by a neuter pronoun, seeing it is a neuter noun. The word *pneuma* did not remain static, but grew in semantic stature through the ages until, in the divine vocabulary, it was given its highest significance. This was also true of *logos*, which once meant simply "word" or "reason." When the Spirit adopted Logos and adapted it to the Word made flesh, it was given personality, and no longer referred merely to a rational concept or to the means of communicating it. So it was with *pneuma*.

In speaking of the Helper who was to take His place, not once did Jesus leave the impression that He was describing a mere breath or influence. Over and over the words "He" and "Him" are used to portray the abilities and functions of the Spirit as a person. Consider, for example, the declaration, "Even the Spirit of truth, whom the world cannot receive, because it neither sees him nor knows him; you know him, for he dwells with you, and will be in you" (John 14:17).

The masculine pronoun *ekeinos* is indicative of a person who can share in the intimacy of fellowship. Those who object to this point out that the term "Spirit of truth" is used as an identification, and implies something besides personality. This is fallacious reasoning when one recalls that the Spirit is often identified by terms depicting His ministry to the saints. There are other expressions, such as the Spirit of life, the Spirit of grace, and the Spirit of promise. In the passage immediately under consideration He is called "the Spirit of truth" because of His ministry through the apostles to the unregenerate world. He was to guide them into all truth, recall for them the truths Jesus had taught them and provide the truth related to things yet to happen. He was not to be a spirit of truth, or truthfulness, in the abstract, but the Spirit through whom saving truth was to be revealed and channeled. He could be known as an abiding presence. The word "know" so often used in the Scripture does not refer to an accumulation of facts about another, but personal identification with him.

A good illustration of this will be found in the words of Jesus, " 'I know my own and my own know me, as the Father knows me, and I know the Father' " (John 10:14, 15). Our experience of the indwelling Spirit is a transcendent life-sharing phenomenon in which the world cannot participate. It belongs only to those who have established a covenant relationship with God, the Spirit being the seal of the covenant.

Those who are inclined to cavil frequently refer to the statement that the world cannot receive the Spirit because it cannot see Him. They ask if the disciples of Christ can see Him, and if not, how they can know that He dwells in them. It may help our understanding to know that the word originally related to men who were appointed as public deputies to attend the games, inspect conditions and participants, to see that all that transpired was legal and orderly. The word did not refer to merely watching, as a spectator in the stands, but to one who looked with interest and purpose.

Because it is unconcerned and indifferent, the world does not see the Spirit. The world occupied with distracting trivia, is insensible to the Spirit's power and pleading. The eyes of the world are closed (Acts 28:27), and the Spirit cannot manifest himself. On the other hand, the person whose heart is open will dwell with Him and be in Him. "With" signifies companionship, while "in" signifies identifying relationship.

In John 16:13-15, the pronouns "he" and "his" occur nine times, in such a context that the personality of the Spirit must certainly be recognized. The Spirit is spoken of as coming, hearing, speaking, recognizing authority, guiding, declaring a message, and glorifying another.

Jesus told the apostles that He was leaving much unsaid because the burden of complete revelation would weigh too heavily upon their hearts. They were in no condition to hear more, lest they be overwhelmed by future responsibility and the suffering that would accompany their ministrations. They were disturbed already by the news that Jesus was leaving them.

"When he comes who is the Spirit of truth, he will guide you into all the truth; for he will not speak on his own authority, but will tell only what he hears; and he will make known to you the things that are coming. He will glorify me, for everything that he makes known to you he will draw from what is mine. All that the Father has is mine, and that is why I said, 'Everything that he makes known to you he will draw from what is mine' " (John 16:13-15; TNEB).[5]

When He comes! This phrase betokens the forthcoming arrival of a person as certainly as it does when used in connection with the advent of Jesus. The Spirit was to accomplish three great objectives: (1) to guide the apostles into all the truth, even to revealing things yet in the future; (2) to glorify Jesus; (3) to be sent by the Father at the request of Jesus, but also to "come" by His own power.

He is the Spirit of truth, that is, truth is His very nature. The revelation can be relied upon. It is authoritative and decisive. The expression "all truth" does not refer to the truth related to all aspects of the universe. It is the truth that redeems and reconciles, and restores the divine-human relationship. The apostles were not yet in a position to receive all details of this saving truth that the Spirit would relay to them. He would do so as they would become able to assimilate and properly apply it.

One who trusts in Jesus can scarcely doubt that the divine design was to vouchsafe to the apostles during their lifetime the full and complete revelation of all that is essential for man to know of his relationship in the kingdom of Heaven. The position of the apostles is unique and they have no successors. Whatever was not revealed during their lifetime is not essential to God's purpose for our lives. Not a single authentic revelation has been given to man since John on Patmos laid down the calamus after

---

[5]From the New English Bible. © the Delegates of the Oxford University Press and the Syndics of the Cambridge University Press 1961, 1970. Reprinted by permission.

writing, "The grace of our Lord Jesus Christ be with you all. Amen"(Revelation 21:21; KJV).

Once more it must be emphasized that the revelation of the Spirit was not given upon the authority of the Spirit. The power of the Spirit to speak is not questioned, but He did not assume the royal prerogative of doing so. The thoughts conveyed were those of the Father, and the Spirit transmitted them with infinite value and faithfulness. The Spirit told the apostles on earth what He had been told to speak from Heaven. His message was not just truthful; it was the truth.

Jesus promised that the Spirit would inform the apostles of what was to come. Those things related to the destiny of the kingdom of Heaven in its encounter with the kingdoms of this world were to be made known as sources of comfort to the saints. The believers would be assured of the final triumph of good over evil, of righteousness over unrighteousness.

This was no new role for the Spirit. He had spoken to and through the prophets of old, warning a profligate people of their fate, revealing to kings and lesser rulers their impending doom. Now, as the divine Helper sent to complete the mission of the Son on earth, He was to gaze through the telescope of the future and see the return of the Lord and the culmination of the divine purpose as it relates to mankind.

Paul was instructed concerning the state of affairs that would obtain in the last days. "The Spirit speaketh expressly, that in the latter times some shall depart from the faith, giving heed to seducing spirits, and doctrines of devils" (1 Timothy 4:1; KJV).

44

He was informed concerning the nature of the resurrected bodies of those who had died, and the transformed bodies of those still alive at the coming of Jesus (1 Corinthians 15:50-57). In the same connection he was told of the ultimate arrangement by which the Son was to deliver the kingdom of God to the Father, so that God could be all in all.

Peter was empowered to write of the certainty of the coming of the day of the Lord, which was to be unexpected as a thief. He also wrote that at that time the "heavens shall pass away with a great noise, and the elements shall melt with fervent heat, and the earth also and the works that are therein shall be burned up" (2 Peter 3:10; KJV).

But John, banished to the isle called Patmos, gazed upon the panorama of the future as it was unrolled. The great sequence of events was paraded to the very end. His divine commission was to "Write the things which thou hast seen, and the things which are, and the things which shall be hereafter" (Revelation 1:19; KJV). He depicts for us in awesome symbols the clash of titanic forces directed from Heaven and from the depths of the abyss. There is the repeated admonition, "He that hath an ear, let him hear what the Spirit saith unto the churches."

If revelation is the unfolding of mystery previously hidden from the discernment of men, surely John's volume is appropriately named. It begins with the narrator watching a door opened in Heaven, and a voice like a trumpet issuing the invitation, "Come up hither, and I will shew the things which must be hereafter." John records the fact, "Immediately I was in the spirit" (Revelation 4:1, 2; KJV). He pens his

45

startling vision, only to conclude, "And he said unto me, These sayings are faithful and true: and the Lord God of the holy prophets sent his angel to shew unto his servants the things which must shortly be done. Behold, I come quickly" (Revelation 22:6, 7; KJV).

The Spirit was also to glorify Jesus. The original for "glorify" is *doxazo*, meaning "to magnify" or "honor." Jesus is the very basis of revelation. All revelation revolves around Him as the center of the moral and spiritual universe. In the solar system the planets revolve around the sun, and in the moral universe all things gain their meaning from the Son of righteousness. "The testimony of Jesus is the spirit of prophecy" (Revelation 19:10).

It is interesting to note that the Spirit would glorify Jesus because everything He would make known to the disciples would have come from Jesus. The original wording should be more correctly rendered, "He will draw from what is mine" (John 16:15; TNEB). It is as if the Spirit were drawing out of a cistern or well of living water to provide sustaining truth to men. While that which is drawn out is sufficient to quench the thirst, it does not exhaust the supply. Much remains to be learned and known when the Son of man comes in the fulness of His glory, accompanied by all of His holy angels. Jesus' statement that the Spirit would draw from what belonged to Jesus is important because it emphasizes the Godhead in its unity. The Father is portrayed as the originator of all things, the Son as the heir of all things, and the Spirit as the revealer of all things ordained for the good of mankind. In Matthew 11:27, Jesus says, "All things are delivered unto me of my

46

Father: and no man knoweth the Son, but the Father; neither knoweth any man the Father, save the Son, and he to whomsoever the Son will reveal him" (KJV).

Any theory of Deity that makes the Son inferior to the Father in glory cannot be sustained by Scripture. God entrusted everything to the Son, and the Spirit glorified the Son by taking from the inexhaustible supply to share it with the apostles, that we in turn might be profited. We glorify the Son in our willing acceptance of the revelation the Spirit gave concerning Him. We dishonor Him when we deny that testimony.

In summarizing the content of this chapter, let us remember that when Jesus spoke of the Spirit He did so in personal terms. He was forced to leave the earthly scene in order to accomplish His purpose. His ascension into Heaven was as important to the divine order as His descent into the earth. It was essential for Him to make intercession at the right hand of God, but He would ask the Father to send another Helper who would make intercession for the saints on earth. This Helper was to be His replacement, and He would function so effectively it would be as if Jesus were still here.

In an interesting statement Jesus said, "Nevertheless I tell you the truth: it is to your advantage that I go away, for if I do not go away, the Counselor will not come to you; but if I go, I will send him to you" (John 16:7). The opening words of this declaration indicate that it would be difficult for the hearers to accept what Jesus said. He reinforced His announcement by insisting that He spoke the truth.

Obviously the apostles would not understand how it could be profitable for Jesus to leave them, so He proceeded to explain that the Spirit would do for them what He could not do by remaining on earth. Moreover, the Spirit would convict the world of sin, righteousness, and judgment, in a manner that could not be done if Jesus remained in the flesh.

All of this points to one conclusion, that Jesus regarded the Spirit as a person, a divine person, and all who desire to imitate Jesus in thought and speech must do the same. Perhaps nothing is more comforting than for one to realize that the divine plan involved an intimate fellowship on earth, first with Jesus dwelling in His body, and second with the Holy Spirit dwelling in our bodies. "Do you not know that your body is the temple of the Holy Spirit within you, which you have from God?" (1 Corinthians 6:19).

4

How Does the Spirit Work?

Our knowledge of the Holy Spirit must come from what the Spirit has revealed concerning himself in the Word of God. I say this in spite of the fact that the view may be unpopular in a time when personal feelings and emotional reactions are frequently considered to be the source of information concerning the nature of the Holy Spirit. This is not to affirm that the Spirit is confined in or to the Word of revelation, nor is it intended to lessen the value of any experiential relationship with the Spirit by the Christian. It does mean that, in revealing the will of God, the Spirit has described and identified himself in such a manner that man can ascertain all that he needs to know about the character of the Spirit in exactly the same way that he learns other aspects of the divine disclosure.

We dare not test or measure the Word of God by personal feelings. We must judge our feelings in the light of God's Word. The ultimate criterion can never be the subjective, but the objective. It is foolish to say, "I do not know what the Word of God says, nor do I care, for I know how I feel." Feelings can be deceptive. One can be as happy when he believes a lie as when he believes the truth. One can be persuaded that a lie is the truth, as every confidence man on earth realizes.

Jeremiah 17 records the judgment of God upon

His people. They are condemned for two things: many persons trusted in men rather than in the Word from Heaven (v. 5); others trusted in their own hearts. "The heart is deceitful above all things, and desperately wicked: who can know it?" (v. 9; KJV). It must be remembered that this is not the evaluation of the prophet, but the declaration of God.

One can be deceived by others, but he can also be deceived by his own heart. This necessitates the twofold warning found in the Scriptures: "Let no man deceive you with vain words" (Ephesians 5:6); "Let no man deceive himself" (1 Corinthians 3:18; KJV). These things are mentioned so that the reader will understand why my appeal is to the revelation of God as we seek to identify the Spirit and to grasp the significance of His work in our world.

I believe the Bible teaches that the Holy Spirit is a divine personality, and it will be my purpose to share with you my reasons for so believing. This is done without apology inasmuch as Jesus said, "It is written, Man shall not live by bread alone, but by every word that proceedeth out of the mouth of God" (Matthew 4:4; KJV).

It is not my intention to become embroiled in the theological donnybrook about the nature and constitution of Deity. I shall be content to speak of Scriptural things in Scriptural terms without inventing or projecting a specialized jargon that tends more to confuse than to enlighten. If it is true that all we know about the nature of God is what has been revealed, and if the revelation has been provided in words, it is apparent that we can find the terms to express any aspect of the divine will.

All thought must be expressed in words to be communicated. If there are no words for a thought, the idea is not there. If, on the other hand, there are words to express the idea, and if all persons accept the words of Scripture as the norm, there can be no division, as long as all men use Scriptural terms to express Scriptural ideas.

An example of what happens when people do not accept the Scripture is found in the use of the term "Trinity." This word does not occur in the Scriptures. It was first used by Tertullian in the second century, and was employed to express a view of the nature of God that was under attack by certain of his contemporaries. Consequently, the brand, *Trinitarians*, was being applied to certain ones, and this, in turn, led to the designation *Unitarians* for the opposers. Both groups considered themselves orthodox expositors of the apostolic doctrine. Yet, if one had asked any apostle if he were a Unitarian or Trinitarian, he would not have understood the question. I shall not belabor the question of whether Deity consists of "three persons in one" or "one person in three."

Matthew speaks of the name of the Father and of the Son and of the Holy Spirit (28:19). Paul writes of the grace of the Lord Jesus Christ and the love of God and the fellowship of the Holy Spirit (2 Corinthians 13:14). One who studies the Bible can determine the functions ascribed to each of these, and from what is taught can reach conclusions as to their respective offices.

Upon this basis I consider the Holy Spirit as a personality. I use the term "personality" rather than "person," although I have no objection to the latter. Our word "person" comes from the Latin word for an actor's mask, and refers to one who enacts a role or performs an individual part in a drama. We still use *persona* to designate a character in a novel or play. The Holy Spirit had a unique part to play in the relationship of Deity to creation, and the sum of the individual qualities and attributes assigned to the Spirit make Him a personality.

Having introduced the word "attributes" we are now prepared to examine the Scriptures and see whether the Spirit is portrayed as an intelligent being in His own right.

The Spirit possesses a mind. "And he who searches the hearts of men knows what is the mind of the Spirit, because the Spirit intercedes for the saints according to the will of God" (Romans 8:27).

This statement occurs in a context of reassurance that God has provided the Spirit to help us in those matters where we show weakness. One such area is that of prayer. We do not know how to pray as we ought. There are deep desires and earnest longings that we cannot express. Our linguistic talents fail us when we try to translate our profound feelings into our limited vocabulary. In such a time "the Spirit himself intercedes for us with sighs too deep for words."

We can be certain that the Father knows the mind of the Spirit and that we are not left to "go it alone." In 1 Corinthians 2:11 we are told that the Spirit knows the mind of God, and in Romans 8:27 we learn that God knows the mind of the Spirit. The mind, or intellect, is the possession of an intelligent being, and this leads us to accept the Spirit as being in that category.

The Holy Spirit can speak and thus communicate thought. Upon this matter there is no room for doubt, if anyone accepts the plain statements of the Scriptures as valid. Occasionally the Spirit took command of human tongues and used them as organs of speech. In Acts 1:16, Peter states, "Men and brethren, this scripture must needs have been fulfilled, which the Holy Ghost by the mouth of David spake before concerning Judas" (KJV). In Acts 4:25, God is given credit for what He "by the mouth of thy servant David hast said." In Acts 28:25, the apostle declares, "Well spake the Holy Ghost by Esaias." In Hebrews 3:7 occurs a citation from Psalm 95:7 with the preface "as the Holy Ghost saith," also in Hebrews is a quotation from Jeremiah 31:33, of which the writer said, "The Holy Ghost also is a witness to us" (10:15-17).

Again, Jesus told the apostles not to be concerned about their defense when they were apprehended and arraigned before governors and kings. He said, "But when they deliver you up, take no thought how or what ye shall speak: for it shall be given you in that same hour what ye shall speak. For it is not ye that speak, but the Spirit of your Father which speaketh in you" (Matthew 10:19, 20; KJV). Notice that both the content and method would be taken care of by the Spirit.

A question that always seems to agitate the minds of men who must "pin things down" and arrive at specifics before they can be happy is the way in which the Spirit has revealed the message of God.

Certain terms have been created to designate the various ideas upon the subject. Some have contended for verbal inspiration, others for thought transference, and the like.

As is frequently the case when we try to capture divine action in human vocabulary, the Spirit may not have been limited to any one theory or any combination. He may well have employed all of them at different times. We know that in old times "men moved by the Holy Spirit spoke from God" (2 Peter 1:21), and we are also told that God spoke in former times through the prophets in different times and in many ways (Hebrews 1:1).

On one occasion the apostle wrote, "Now the Spirit speaketh expressly," that is, exactly or precisely. This is an indication that at other times the speaking was done with less directness; however, we must never develop a theory that eliminates the use of words in the communication of the Spirit. The Holy Spirit employed language known to men and used by them in their social interchange; otherwise, what was conveyed would not have been a revelation at all. If the language employed was an esoteric or secret code, the subject would have remained a mystery. This is the exact opposite of revelation.

On the Day of Pentecost the Spirit came to provide visual and audible proof that Jesus had been exalted to the right hand of God and had received of the Father the promised Holy Spirit. Through the apostles He testified to wonderful works of God. He communicated this testimony through the native languages of the hearers who were present "from every nation under heaven." Those who spoke in "other languages," that is, in languages they had not learned, did so "as the Spirit gave them utterance."

No revelation has been given to man except in the language of man, that is, as relates to the obligations and duties of man. Nothing else could be regarded as a revelation. It is true that because of the multiplicity of languages used by peoples, tribes, and nations, translation is necessary to make the message understandable to those who did not receive it directly. Revelation is one thing, and translation is another, however.

In the previous chapter, mention was made of Paul's original encounter with the residents of Corinth. This city, the center of commercialized vice in the ancient world, was a veritable showcase exhibiting the fruits of human wisdom coupled with idolatry.

Into this maelstrom of human wickedness entered one who confessed that he came "in weakness and in much fear and trembling." He came bearing the good news that the living God had visited the earth in the form of a Son, and that message was presented in words of stark simplicity. It was a matter of allowing the facts to speak for themselves. Paul intimates that he had the power of deciding his approach to a given culture. He could have used the philosophic method. He was familiar with the teachings of the pagan world, for he quoted from Cleanthes, Epimenides, and others, at various times. But he chose to decry the wisdom of "the rulers of this transitory age" and to impart the wisdom that "God decreed before the ages for our glorification."

This wisdom has to be revealed. It could not be

learned by visual or audible methods, because it was beyond the power of the senses to ascertain. Nor could it be learned by rationalization. It was outside the realm of deduction for finite minds. It could be revealed only by the Holy Spirit. It bore no resemblance to the spirit of the age, because that spirit knows nothing of the purpose and pleasure of God.

We are told that the Spirit used words for communicating the things freely given of God. "Which things also we speak, not in the words which man's wisdom teacheth, but which the Holy Ghost teacheth" (1 Corinthians 2:13; KJV). Surely it requires an intellectual being to select and employ a vocabulary to transmit divine thought to human mentality. The Spirit possesses a mind to accumulate divine information and the ability to share it.

The Holy Spirit can testify to fact and bear witness to men and through men. This is made clear in Jesus' talk with His disciples just before His betrayal and crucifixion. These men were sad because Jesus had told them He was to leave them and return to the Father. They had forsaken everything in order to follow Him. They had been His constant companions for three or more years. The contemplation of a life without this Friend was almost unthinkable. Jesus pointed out to them that He would compensate for their grief and loneliness by requesting the Father to send them another Helper, a Companion who would remain although He himself was absent. In direct language He identified this advocate as the Holy Spirit, and informed them of some of the things the Spirit would accomplish and provide. He reassured them with these words: "But when the Comforter is come, whom I will send unto you from the Father, even the Spirit of truth, which proceedeth from the Father, he shall testify of me: and ye also shall bear witness, because ye have been with me from the beginning" (John 15:26, 27; KJV). The Holy Spirit was to come and bear witness to the culmination of the divine purpose: that all authority should be granted to the Son, and He would occupy a seat at the right hand of God. The apostles were witnesses to the personal ministry of Jesus from its beginning. The Spirit descended upon Jesus to inaugurate His personal witness to the world. The same Spirit would descend upon the apostles to inaugurate their witness to the world.

In many respects the apostolic mission was the mission of the Spirit, the apostles being the agents. The Spirit would act as a teacher and guide, assuring perfect recall of the precepts of Jesus. "But the Comforter, which is the Holy Ghost, whom the Father will send in my name, he shall teach you all things, and bring all things to your remembrance, whatsoever I have said unto you" (John 14:26; KJV).

An analysis of this statement may be helpful. The Spirit was to be sent by the Father, but in the name of Jesus. This last expression indicates the authority under which the Spirit would operate. At the accession of Jesus to the throne, all authority was conferred on Him, and He will continue to exercise it until the last enemy has been destroyed. Any divine action taken in the kingdom of Heaven must be under the authority of the Son.

The Holy Spirit has no direct authority, but acts or functions by derivative authority. All authority was invested in the Father until it was transferred to the Son (1 Corinthians 15:27). The Spirit does nothing in His own name, that is, upon His own authority.

Another point of interest is that the Spirit was to make use of the rational powers of the human messengers of Jesus. It is certainly true that upon occasion, and in emergency, the Spirit commandeered the tongues of the apostles to speak words of defense with no thought required by the speaker. Such involuntary speech was certainly rendered when the apostles were unjustly arraigned before kings and magistrates. But the Spirit also taught them, and this involves a learning process requiring cooperation upon the part of the student. In addition to the faculty of perception, that of memory was also stimulated so that those who had been with Jesus could recall the things He had taught. Later this would be designated "the gift of knowledge."

The promise to the apostles was amplified by another statement of Jesus: "Howbeit when he, the Spirit of truth, is come, he will guide you into all truth: for he shall not speak of himself; but whatsoever he shall hear, that shall he speak: and he will shew you things to come. He shall glorify me: for he shall receive of mine, and shall shew it unto you" (John 16:13, 14; KJV).

"All truth" refers to the body of truth of divine revelation, that which is required to save and sanctify men. It was such truth the apostles were commissioned to furnish the world, and which they were to receive from the Spirit. The expression, "for he shall not speak of himself," is frequently misunderstood and misapplied. It is taken to mean that the Spirit will say nothing about himself, His influence, or function. This cannot be true because the Scriptures furnish us much material about the Holy Spirit. If the Spirit had not spoken about himself we would have known nothing about His work.

The expression here does not mean that the Spirit will say nothing about himself, rather that He will not speak upon His own authority. This passage is clear even in the *King James Version* when properly considered, "He shall not speak of himself; *but whatsoever he shall hear, that shall he speak.*" The thought is that the Spirit is the agent for, not the source of, the testimony. *The Revised Version* and *New English Bible* are correct in rendering the expression, "For he will not speak on his own authority."

It must be noted that the Spirit was not only to bring to memory the things Jesus had taught in the past, but was also to reveal future things. Jesus had to forgo dealing with many things because His disciples were not yet able to bear them (John 16:12). The word translated "bear" means literally, "to lift up for the purpose of carrying." Metaphorically it signifies one's taking up thoughts or assimilating concepts. In subsequent revelation the Spirit disclosed many things that were to transpire. One such record is called The Revelation, or *Apocalypse*. It actually portrays the future of the kingdom of the heavens and the kingdoms of this world.

The Spirit would glorify Jesus, in that every disclosure that was made would be drawn from Jesus, the embodiment of all wisdom and power. Jesus made this clear. "All that the Father has is mine; therefore I said that he will take what is mine and declare it to you" (John 16:15; RSV). It is evident that the Spirit was to be the earthly advocate or helper during the time Jesus reigned by the will of the Father. It seems equally evident that the witness borne by the Spirit was to be personal, teaching, reminding, and foretelling future events. These are not the actions of a vague influence, but of an individual, divine and prescient.

The Spirit is credited with selecting and calling men to fulfill certain missions. The congregation of saints in Antioch of Syria was fortunate in having a number of prophets and teachers in its service. "While they were worshiping the Lord and fasting, the Holy Spirit said, 'Set apart for me Barnabas and Saul for the work to which I have called them.' Then after fasting and praying they laid their hands on them and sent them off" (Acts 13:2, 3).

It is interesting to note that while they were sent forth by the congregation, Luke also gives credit to the Holy Spirit. "So, being sent out by the Holy Spirit, they went down to Seleucia; and from there they sailed to Cyprus" (v. 4). That the Spirit mapped out their route and determined the places they were to visit is strongly suggested in Acts 16:6: "And they went through the region of Phrygia and Galatia, having been forbidden by the Holy Spirit to speak the word in Asia." From this it appears that the Holy Spirit is a personality regulating and arranging the work of apostolic mission, exercising control over both time and place for the initial proclamation of the good news in various places. We, being human and limited in both knowledge and insight, are not always capable of judging the opportune time in which to present our witness to a people; but the Spirit, knowing the hearts of men, is able to judge.

The Spirit is portrayed as possessing will and acting accordingly. Three chapters of Paul's first letter to the Corinthians are dedicated to a discussion of special gifts of the Holy Spirit. This was made imperative because of strife, especially over misuse of the ability granted to some to speak in other languages (1 Corinthians 12—14). In 12:7 Paul points out that the gifts are distributed to various members of the body, and each one who receives a manifestation of the Spirit is to use it for the common good.

There follows a catalogue of the nine spiritual gifts, all of which were apparently possessed by individuals in that congregation. The apostle then writes: "All these are inspired by one and the same Spirit, who apportions to each one individually as he wills" (v. 11). It is clear that in the distribution of gifts the decision as to who should receive them remained with the Spirit. Regardless of how eager one might be to receive a special gift, the final apportionment was not dependent upon the will of the recipient, but upon the will of the Spirit.

An interesting observation about the origin of prophecy occurs in 2 Peter 1:21, where the apostle asserts that the things spoken and written by godly men of old did not result from an interpretation of events by the prophets themselves. They did not observe what was going on and deduce their prophecies from their views of what might lie ahead as a result. They spoke as they were motivated by the

Holy Spirit. The Holy Spirit determined both the appropriate time and content of prophetic declarations. In this the human will of the mouthpiece was made subservient to the will of the Spirit.

A summary of what has been said in this chapter will remind us that the Holy Spirit possesses a mind, and can communicate thought. Moreover, the Spirit can testify to what has been said by another, guide listeners into truth, men into certain missions, and exercise will in selecting those who are to be recipients of special gifts and qualifying abilities.

Again, it must be emphasized that these are attributes of a person and can hardly be assigned to a mere influence or a vague, motivating force. This means that if one is to share in the life of the Spirit he must become a partaker of the divine life—the life of God—in a genuine personal relationship. This is the distinguishing characteristic between the one who recognizes Jesus as Lord over his life and the one who rejects His lordship. One's acceptance of Christ makes the difference between life and death.

5

How Is the Spirit Related to God?

One cannot always judge a person by those with whom he is associated. Sometimes a grave injustice is wrought by attempting to do so. But I think a legitimate conclusion to reach with reference to the Holy Spirit is that He is both a person and is divine. He is repeatedly mentioned in direct conjunction with two divine persons, with no qualifying statement indicating that He is different. The conclusion is bolstered by the connections in which the combinations occur and by the functions performed by each of the principals.

For the sake of brevity we will confine ourselves in this chapter to the New Covenant Scriptures. A good place to begin is in conjunction with the incarnation. Gabriel was sent to Mary from God (Luke 1:26). He assured the virgin that the Lord was with her. He quieted her fears by telling her that she had found favor with God. She was then told that she would be impregnated by the Holy Spirit. "The Holy Ghost shall come upon thee, . . . therefore also that holy thing which shall be born of thee shall be called the Son of God" (Luke 1:35; KJV).

In this instance we have God, the Holy Spirit, and the Son of God. It is the Father who wills, the Spirit being the executive agent, the conveyor of life. Nothing about the fertilization of a human ovum by a divine seed, or life-giving principle, should cause doubt to one who believes in the creation of man by God. In the beginning the breath of God, breathed into an elemental body taken from the dust of the earth, made human life possible. In one sense, the only life we have is the result of the divine and human, and all of us by nature are sons of God. If the first Adam became a living being by the divine breath, it is not strange that the second Adam began His earthly mission by a union of the divine and human.

We do not need to understand or be able to explain fully the varied roles of the principals involved in the birth of Jesus to realize that the Father, the Spirit, and the Son all had distinctive parts in the drama of the ages. The means may remain a mystery while we accept the fact upon faith. When Mary submitted herself to the will of God with the words of resignation, "Be it unto me according to thy word," her womb became the depository of the divine seed, and that meant that the Son of God was sent forth to be "made of a woman, made under the law" (Galatians 4:4; KJV).

We turn now from the advent of Jesus to His final commission to the twelve before His ascension to Heaven. As Matthew records it, after the resurrection of Jesus the eleven apostles journeyed northward to Galilee. They gathered on a mountain where He had promised to meet them. When they saw Him they worshiped Him, although some felt that "it was too good to be true." Then Jesus revealed that all authority was granted Him in Heaven and on earth, a way of explaining the universality of the lordship bestowed upon Him by the Father. This empowered

Him to send them forth as ambassadors to all nations of men. The *Authorized Version* renders His words, "Go ye therefore, and teach all nations, baptizing them in the name of the Father, and of the Son, and of the Holy Ghost: teaching them to observe all things whatsoever I have commanded you" (Matthew 28:19, 20).

Once again we have found the Holy Spirit appearing in relationship with the Father and the Son, and in such a connection that a clear distinction is to be made between the three, although such unity is manifested that the word "name" appears in the singular.

We turn attention next to Ephesians 4:4-6, where Paul enumerates the seven "ones" upon which our unity is conditioned and must be maintained. The immediate context expresses concern that those who are called conduct themselves in a manner that will bring honor upon that calling. Since we have been called into unity with Christ, nothing reflects against that calling more than strife and division. Of all people on this earth, those who are in Christ Jesus should be most harmonious.

In order to maintain oneness, four essentials are recommended: lowliness, meekness, longsuffering, and forbearance in love. The first of these is better represented by our word "humility." It must be remembered that in the world surrounding Ephesus this was not regarded as a virtue. Humility implied cowering and cringing under servility, or slavishness. Jesus clothed this term with beauty and grace by His own sacrifice and service. He humbled himself to come in the form of a servant and became obedient unto death, even the death on the cross. In this light, humility took on a completely new color. It was no longer regarded as an indication of weakness, but of genuine strength and power. E. H. Chapin said, "Humility is not a weak and timid quality; it must be carefully distinguished from a groveling spirit. There is such a thing as an honest pride and self-respect. Though we may be servants of all, we should be servile to none."[6]

Humility is as essential to the maintenance of unity as breath is to life. When one knows his qualifications and abilities, and yet is willing to step down in favor of another who may not have the same potential; when he is qualified to play first violin, but is willing to "play second fiddle" so that harmony will prevail in the orchestra, unity will generally be preserved. Humility recognizes its rights, but refuses to assert or insist upon them, realizing that rights are secondary to responsibilities.

"Meekness," in its original Greek form, is full of beauty that cannot be completely captured in any single word in our English language. Any correct understanding of it must begin with the recognition that meekness is not weakness, but just the opposite. Many centuries ago a Christian wrote, "The meek are not those who are never at all angry, for such are insensible; but those who, feeling anger, control it, and are angry only when they ought to be. Meekness excludes revenge, irritability, morbid sensitiveness, but not self-defense, or a quiet and steady

---

[6]Tryon Edwards, *Useful Quotations* (New York: Grosset and Dunlap, 1933), p. 267.

maintenance of right."[7] It is doubtful that any modern writer could give a better description of the quality called "meekness."

Nothing else is more likely to cause strife and contention than impatience coupled with a short temper. The word for "longsuffering" is *makrothumia*, a combined form of *makros*, long, and *thumos*, temper. Certainly it is associated with endurance under pressure, but it is interesting to know that it never occurs in the Greek classics. The virtue it represents was unknown to the poets and philosophers, or was despised by them as unmanly. So the word can be regarded as one given meaning or content by the life and teachings of Jesus.

The reason for this is easily seen when it is recognized that *makrothumia* was first a characteristic of God, who patiently endured and put up with human shortcomings in order to work good. The longsuffering of God waited in the days of Noah while the ark was being prepared. God is long-suffering toward us, not willing that any should perish. The gods of the Romans and Greeks were conceived as vengeful and spiteful. Since people are like their gods, it is understandable why longsuffering is an attribute of Christians rather than pagans.

Impatience, the enemy of the trusting heart, upsets the mental equilibrium, chafes the spirit, and destroys all inner tranquillity. It is an irritant enflaming the mind and erupting in open criticism mingled

---

[7]Theophylactus, Archbishop of the Bulgarians (1107), *Commentary on Acts and Epistles of Paul*, F. Morellus, ed. (Paris, 1631).

with the gall of bitterness. Ralph Waldo Emerson, who wrote much about patience, declared that patience coupled with fortitude conquers all things. He urged all men to adopt the pace of nature, declaring that her secret is patience. It is unwise to allow the corrosion of impatience to rust the hinges of the heart so that when the blessing is delivered it cannot open the door to receive it.

Closely allied to patience is the word "forbearing," from *anecho*, or "hold back." It describes the person who does not give vent to hurtful expressions, that is, one who restrains himself from actions that antagonize or intensify feelings. We are to bear one another in love, not allowing shortcomings or failures to cause us to explode in anger or recrimination.

All of these qualities are emphasized as essential to those who are "eager to maintain the unity of the Spirit in the bond of peace." Unity is not created by these attitudes, great and noble though they may be. Unity is received from God and not achieved by man. It is a gift of the Spirit. "Maintain" is from a word meaning "to guard, watch, or preserve." It was used twice to describe the action of the four squads of soldiers detailed to guard Peter while in prison (Acts 12:5, 6). The unity of the Spirit has been entrusted to us, placed in our custody, and we are under divine orders to keep it, lest it inadvertently slip away while we are off guard.

The restraining force by which we can keep the unity of the Spirit is the bond of peace. To the extent that we disturb or weaken the peace we lessen the hold we have upon unity. When peace flies out the window unity leaves by the door. The four personal qualities prescribed are not given in order to maintain unity, but to strengthen the bond of peace, which binds unity within the framework of our association. Our calling is to exhibit and manifest the unity God has ordained as His ultimate purpose only in Christ Jesus.

Seven units in that unity are gifts of the Spirit. All of them are provided by divine wisdom and are to be received by us as essential to the eternal design. Not one of these provides for any question as to its existence or validity. It is not that there ought to be one body, one Spirit, and one hope, but *they are*. It is not that there should be one Lord, one faith, and one baptism, but *they are*. Their existence is not contingent upon human understanding or discovery. They are integral parts of the given unity, the unity of the Spirit. Perhaps that is why the one Spirit is mentioned before the other members of the Deity.

By one Spirit, one faith, one baptism, we are brought into relationship of the one Lord, welded together in the one body and made partakers of the one hope. All of this is according to the will of one God and Father whose personality penetrates the entire arrangement.

A powerful argument for the oneness of all the believers is here presented, and is enhanced by the harmony between the one Father, one Lord, and one Spirit. In spite of their divergent functions they are one in nature and purpose. Since we are indwelt by the one Spirit, we should work together. It is appropriate to have impressed upon us first of all the attributes essential to the maintenance of unity, and then learn that the unity of the Spirit involves Heaven as well as earth.

Another illustration of the association of the Spirit with the Father and Son is found in the treatment of spiritual gifts, the *charismata*, possessed by the saints in Corinth. The congregation planted in this center of Gentile profligacy was fortunate to have had the ministrations of Paul. He refers to them as "my workmanship in the Lord," and writes, "If to others I am not an apostle, at least I am to you; for you are the seal of my apostleship in the Lord" (1 Corinthians 9:2).

From the very beginning the Corinthians were accustomed to those demonstrations which constituted divine credentials, confirming the apostolic message as of heavenly origin. All truth must be rendered credible before it can be believed. Credibility can be established only by evidence. Natural truths may be sustained by natural evidence, but supernatural truth requires supernatural validation. So Paul reminded the Corinthians "The signs of a true apostle were performed among you in all patience, with signs and wonders and mighty works" (2 Corinthians 12:12).

When the apostle was forced to move on to other fields of labor at the call of the Spirit, he did not leave the Corinthians without divine assistance, but conferred upon them gifts of speech and knowledge, in the same manner he had confirmed his own proclamation. "In every way you were enriched in him with all speech and all knowledge—even as the testimony to Christ was confirmed among you—so that you are not lacking in any spiritual gift, as you wait for the revealing of our Lord Jesus Christ who will sustain you to the end" (1 Corinthians 1:5-8).

Unfortunately, those who were invested with the gifts became proud of their possession, and began to abuse them by diverting them from their true purpose. It became necessary for Paul to recall them to a more responsible attitude. We dare not rejoice over their malpractice, but we can still benefit from what was said in correcting the error, and we must not forget to profit by their mistakes.

It is interesting to note that Paul began the section of the Corinthian letter relating to spiritual gifts with the words, "Now concerning spiritual gifts, brethren, I would not have you ignorant" (1 Corinthians 12:1; KJV). The word "gifts" is not in the original, and a literal rendering would probably be "spiritual things"; however, the information that follows leaves no doubt that the subject is the special endowments, that is, the gifts of the Spirit.

The expression "I would not have you ignorant" points up the fact that acquisition of knowledge in matters of the Spirit is the will of Him who sent the Spirit. The same expression is used with reference to things, such as Paul's purpose and intention with regard to Rome (Romans 1:13), the persecution suffered because of his preaching in Asia Minor (2 Corinthians 1:8), God's design as related to Israel (Romans 11:25), and the resurrection of the sleeping saints (1 Thessalonians 4:13). When God furnishes information, refusal to learn is inexcusable.

Obviously, God does not want us to continue with unused mental capacities. Ignorance is not bliss! It is also apparent that if God does not want us to be ignorant about a subject, the information He supplies will be adequate. An examination of the revelation related to spiritual gifts will show that we are supplied facts concerning their origin, variety, purpose, function, and regulation.

It is important to remember that the dispelling of ignorance concerning spiritual gifts was not left to those who had the gifts, but as assumed by the apostle who put it in writing. The Corinthians came behind in no gift, but "to one [was] given by the Spirit the word of wisdom; to another the word of knowledge by the same Spirit" (1 Corinthians 12:8; KJV). If the gifts were self-validating and instructive, the Corinthian congregation would have required no apostolic letter upon the subject. Yet, to this congregation the written message was sent. Hence, those who would not be ignorant concerning spiritual gifts should turn to the apostolic letter for instruction and guidance. The saints in Corinth who possessed the gifts were ignorant of their purpose and function, otherwise this portion of the letter was superfluous.

After declaring he would not have them ignorant about spiritual gifts, Paul wrote, "Ye know that ye were Gentiles, carried away unto these dumb idols, even as ye were led" (v. 2; KJV). The real problem at Corinth was created by those who had the gift of speaking various kinds of tongues. They had exercised this gift in such a manner that unbelievers dropping in upon the assembly could have concluded they were insane.

The Corinthians had been idolaters, having grown up in a pagan culture. The apostle mentions that they had been carried away to dumb idols.

Graven images could not speak. Molten gods could provide no message or revelation. But the living God could not only reveal His thoughts, but could also empower His servants to convey His words in "other tongues." So overjoyed were the former heathen that theirs was a speaking God, they could hardly restrain themselves.

Men respond according to the spirit that motivates them. In 1 Corinthians 2:12, the apostle contrasts the spirit of that age with the Spirit of God. The Corinthians had paid homage to dumb idols even as they had been led. The spirit of the decadent age influenced them in their devotion, but Paul gave them to understand that no one "speaking by the Spirit of God calleth Jesus accursed: And that no man can say that Jesus is the Lord, but by the Holy Ghost" (1 Corinthians 12:3; KJV).

To say that Jesus is Lord constituted a much more serious responsibility in the Roman Empire than it does today. Rome was regarded as tolerant of the religious beliefs of the provinces, and well she might be, because she regarded them all as harmless superstition. While this was true, one thing was required. Annually, on the birthday of the emperor, every citizen had to appear in the marketplace before the bust of Caesar, burn a pinch of incense, and publicly affirm "Caesar is lord." This presented no particular problem to the pagans who believed in a multiplicity of deities. The Roman Senate had officially elevated Caesar to the pantheon and declared him to be divine. His character, while certainly not godlike, was like that of the other gods.

The one group in the Empire whose members

could not freely join the populace in hailing Caesar was the community of the reconciled. The apostle states the problem clearly: "There be that are called gods, whether in heaven or in earth (as there be gods many, and lords many,) but to us there is but one God, the Father, of whom are all things, and we in him; and one Lord Jesus Christ, by whom are all things, and we by him" (1 Corinthians 8:5, 6; KJV). The problem was complicated by another requirement of any person brought under suspicion. If an accusation was filed against him concerning his faith in Caesar, the magistrates were to bring him before the statue and demand a public affirmation under penalty of death or banishment from family and friends. If the accused was suspected of belonging to the despised followers of Christ, he was required, in addition to his affirmation of the lordship of Caesar, to announce, "Anathema Jesus," that is, "Jesus is accursed." So to say that Jesus was Lord might well be a matter of life and death. Preserved for us is a remarkable document alluding to this very matter, a letter written by Pliny the Younger to the Emperor Trajan, near the beginning of the second century. Pliny was appointed governor of Bithynia. Never having had to cope with the problem of Christians, he wrote to gain information as to the proper procedure to follow. If you have not read his letter it will be interesting to do so. Here it is:

"Having never been present at any trials of the Christians, I am unacquainted as to the methods and limits to be observed in examining and punishing them. Whether, therefore, any difference is to be made with respect to age, or no distinction is to be observed between the young and adult; whether repentance admits to a pardon; or if a man has been once a Christian, it avails him nothing to recant; whether the mere profession of Christianity, albeit without any criminal act, or only the crimes associated therewith are punishable; in all these points I am greatly doubtful. In the meanwhile the method I have observed towards those who have been denounced to me as Christians, is this; I interrogated them whether they were Christians; if they confessed I repeated the question twice again, adding a threat of capital punishment; if they still persevered, I ordered them to be executed. For I was persuaded, that whatever the nature of their creed, a contumacious and inflexible obstinacy certainly deserved chastisement. There were others also brought before me possessed with the same infatuation; but being citizens of Rome, I directed them to be carried thither.

"These accusations, from the mere fact that the matter was being investigated, began to spread, and several forms of the mischief came to light. A placard was posted up without any signature, accusing a number of people by name. Those who denied that they were Christians, or had ever been so, who repeated after me an invocation to the gods, and offered religious rites with wine and frankincense to your statue (which I had ordered to be brought for the purpose, together with those of the gods), and finally cursed the name of Christ (none of which it is said, those who are really Christians can be forced into performing), I thought it proper to discharge. Others who were named by the informer, at first confessed themselves Christians, and then denied it; true, they had been of that persuasion formerly, but had now quitted it (some three years, others many years, and a few as much as twenty-five years ago). They all worshiped your statue, and the images of the gods, and cursed the name of Christ."[8]

It was for just such a crisis that the Spirit was given as Comforter, an inner source of strength, so that men might glorify Christ in death as well as in life. When Jesus promised to send the Spirit He said, "He will glorify me." Caesar had his legions willing to die with his name upon their lips, and if the Lord of life could not trust those who had enlisted under the banner of faith to do the same, His cause was lost. Thus, the acclamation "Jesus is Lord," while the Roman lictors stood guard ready to flay the flesh from the body with their rods, or to sever the head with the axe, was not only a test of one's faith in the lordship of Jesus, but a proof of the indwelling Spirit. Men act according to the spirit that motivates them.

No man speaking by the Spirit of God would say "anathema Jesus," as even the Roman governor of Bithynia bore witness. Neither could a man make the public declaration that Jesus is the Lord except by the help of the Spirit who dwelt in him. It is interesting to note that the term "Spirit of God" is here used interchangeably with "Holy Spirit."

After this introduction the apostle affirms that various gifts and functions were to be performed by their use, but all of these had a common origin. "There are varieties of gifts, but the same Spirit" (1 Corinthians 12:4). The whole tenor of the chapter is

---

[8]Pliny the Younger, Governor of Bithynia (Epistle X. 97),

the unity that should prevail in the body of Christ. Inasmuch as the body must supply many needs and perform diverse functions, gifts were imparted of such a number and nature as to enable the body to fulfill its mission. God is a divine economist. He did not create needs and then supply gifts to meet them, but needs existed and He created gifts to meet them.

We can be certain that the saints did not lack anything essential to their fulfilling their role upon earth. We can be just as sure that every gift was to be utilized in such a manner as to edify or build up the whole. The exercise of the gifts must not be divisive, for the Spirit is one. Nine gifts are mentioned, and these were given to encourage and stimulate the body to act as God had ordained.

"There are varieties of service, but the same Lord" (v. 5). The original term for "service" is *diakonia*, sometimes translated "ministry." This may be misleading in our day when ministry is regarded as the domain of one man hired by a congregation as its minister. No such specialized meaning was applied to it by the apostles. Every Christian is a minister, and every form of service is part of the ministry. Various ministries are to be carried out and each is essential and commissioned by the same Lord.

"And there are varieties of working, but it is the same God who inspires them all in every one" (v. 6). God works in His saints, Christ directs the work into meaningful forms of service, and the Spirit empowers and enables the saints to fulfill their varied tasks. A difference exists between the Holy Spirit, Christ, and God, and yet a profound unity is involved in them. Surely the Spirit is as much a divine personality as the other two.

One of the most beautiful statements of Paul is his closing sentence to the Corinthians, in 2 Corinthians 13:14. The setting lends interest to the reading. He pointed out that if he should return to Corinth he would not spare any of those who had sinned. His stated intention was to give full proof to all who questioned that Christ was speaking through him. He held forth the hope that the Corinthians would abstain from evil, not because of a desire to gain approval for his own work, but to establish their own moral integrity. He urged them to be "perfect, be of good comfort, be of one mind, live in peace; and the God of love and peace shall be with you" (2 Corinthians 13:11; KJV).

In spite of the agonizing problems in the congregation, the apostle concludes with the words that have often been repeated as a benediction: "The grace of the Lord Jesus Christ, and the love of God, and the communion of the Holy Ghost, be with you all. Amen" (v. 14). The breakdown of these three blessings is important. It was not by accident that the various attributes were credited as they were.

"Grace" is a good example of a term into which the Spirit breathed and infused new life. The result is that any attempt to define it serves only to confine it. Our verbal garb acts as a straitjacket. The consequence is that many who parrot a definition think they understand grace, when all they do is to underestimate it. Grace is not so much to be explained as to be experienced. God is not so much concerned that we experience a share of grace as He is that we share in the experience of grace. That experience relates to the eternal purpose from the moment of its inception and on through the ages of ages. As is so often the case, a study of the derivation constitutes the best definition, for the evolution of the term made it a "vessel fit for the Master's use." In the beginning, *charis* referred to charm, an inner quality resulting in what we refer to as personal magnetism or admirable skill. That kind of concern for others manifested itself in proper decorum under all circumstances, politeness, and deference mingled with understanding of others. We revert to this original use when we speak of those who possess *charisma*, that attractiveness which draws others to them. It is what we mean when we speak of a graceful person, or one who is gracious.

With the passing of time *charis* took on a deeper meaning. The quality the word described was not attained by study or striving, but seemed to be inherent. It was thus assumed to be a gift of the gods, enabling certain individuals to stand out from the multitude. The sculptor whose skill could draw forth figures from marble was said to posses a *charism* for carving. The orator whose use of words was powerful enough to make men alternately laugh and weep was thought to possess the *charism* of speech or rhetoric. We still speak of persons who are gifted in the same manner.

Charisma seemed to be present in an individual from earliest childhood, before he had exerted any effort to secure it. Thus the ancients deemed that it was a gift of a god, unearned and undeserved, empowering one to fulfill the purpose for which destiny had marked him out. Any failure to fulfill the responsibility entailed by the gift was an insult to the deity that bestowed the gift.

By the time Jesus came to earth the word *charis* had come to refer to an undeserved gift, bestowed by a deity, for the purpose of helping to fulfill the ideal of the gods among men. It is no wonder that the Spirit adopted a term so pregnant with meaning and endowed it with a richness it never before possessed. From a gift bestowed by an imaginary god it came to mean that quality in the living God which motivated Him to share himself with sinful men.

Grace reached its apex in Jesus, who emptied himself and took on the form of a slave that He might share in the life of men doomed to die. The grace of the Lord Jesus Christ is not simply something that He gave to men or bestowed upon them. It embraces the whole arrangement by which He agreed to abide with us in our suffering that we might someday share in His glory. The greatest gift of Jesus to the world is himself.

In direct conjunction with the grace of Christ is mentioned the love of God. It is a philosophic question whether grace was prompted by love, or love by grace. It is true that the important thing is to be recipients of these blessings whether or not one ever has a clear concept of their metaphysical relationship. My personal conviction is that grace grows out of and is a fruit of love. This is based upon the fact that God is love. This is His essence. Grace is the benevolence applying that love to fallen man. It is God's moving into the human realm and sharing himself without restraint or limitation.

"Love" is our translation of *agape* (ah-gah-pay), one of four words for love found in the Greek language. The others were too limited in scope and nature to be employed in describing the love God had for us and we must have for one another. *Agape* is not a classical word, and was not found in the writings of the great philosophers. Why did the Spirit select it and reject the others? One reason is that the other terms generally describe an emotion. They have to do with an involuntary feeling of the heart. Emotions are spontaneous reactions to situations or conditions. They require no conscious effort and do not occur as a result of our searching or seeking. They belong to the heart and its passions.

Agape is not an emotion, although it involves the emotions. It is a state resulting from an act of will, a deliberate choice of the mind. One cannot speak of "falling in love" when talking about *agape*, because it is not something into which you tumble. It is a vital, active principle of life. There is a difference between falling when you cannot help it, and stooping down to share the lot of another. Jesus did not become the Son of man because He fell in love with us, for He did not fall at all. Because He loved us He stooped down to participate with us in the human predicament.

Agape represents an achievement of the mind, a victory attained by determination. It is a conquest over one's nature. This is obvious when it is realized that no one can love his enemies until selfishness is vanquished and he has conquered every natural inclination and desire.

Other forms of love see the good or value in a

person or thing and love because of it. *Agape* creates its own sense of values by the very act or process of loving. Under other kinds of love a thing is loved because of its value; in *agape* it is valued because it is loved. God loved us when we were alienated and hostile, hating Him and hating one another. Nothing in us was loving or lovable, but because we were loved we were made deserving. "God commendeth his love toward us, in that, while we were yet sinners, Christ died for us" (Romans 5:8; KJV).

Agape, like *charis*, can never be fully defined in words developed for human communication. To reduce it to words is to imprison it in a finite conception. In the very act of imprisoning it, it escapes us. All that we can do is to create a working statement by which we will be able to measure our own concept of love, rather than measuring love itself. My own rather feeble mental approach to it can be stated as follows: *Agape* is that active and beneficent goodwill which stops at nothing to serve the good of the beloved object.

Love bestowed to elicit or receive a response is prompted more by the need of the giver than the receiver. It is not a benefaction, but an investment. Noteworthy is the fact that love originated with One who had no need and is always outgoing toward those whose needs are great. We are told that God is love, but we are also told that "love is of God."

The love we share for others is not really our love at all. We become channels for the love of God. The water flowing through the pipes into our homes does not belong to the conduits through which it is pumped. Likewise the love flowing like a fountain through us is not ours. It is poured out into our hearts by the Holy Spirit.

This brings us to the third item in the benediction to the saints at Corinth: the communion of the Holy Spirit. Remember that it is connected with the majestic terms, grace and love. This very association is indicative of the manner in which God regards it. Grace, love, and fellowship—these constitute a triad of blessings associated with the greatest names in the universe. It is a matter of great importance that the apostle closes his epistle to the distressed and distressful congregation at Corinth with such a benediction.

The word here for "communion" is *koinonia*, generally translated "fellowship." Most lexicographers agree, however, that it is a word of such depth that no single English term can exhaust its meaning. This becomes evident when we realize the variety of terms for it occurring in the *King James Version*. The root word means "*common*," indicating something shared or held in common. From it we derive such words as "community."

What is the fellowship of the Spirit? Certainly it is not something men attain or achieve by their own merit or efforts. Just as grace is bestowed by Christ and love is bestowed by God, so fellowship is a gift of the Spirit. We share in grace, love, and life as blessings from Heaven. The very best definition of fellowship is "the sharing of a common life," and the *New English Bible* so translates *koinonia*.

The fellowship, or communion, of which the apostle writes is not the mere participation with others in common pursuits. Men may pool their resources and combine their efforts without recourse to the Spirit at all. History is filled with misguided attempts of atheistic social reformers to create colonies where the name of God was proscribed and reading of the Bible was prohibited. The common life in which we are to share is the life of the Spirit.

To substitute the term "share the life of the Spirit" for the term "communion [fellowship] of the Spirit" still does not answer the question as to what is meant by, or involved in, the life of the Spirit. In the New Covenant Scriptures the word *koinonia* is found twenty times. It is rendered "fellowship" twelve times in the *King James Version*, which also translates it "communion" four times. Of the twelve times it is translated "fellowship," one-third of these occur in 1 John 1. In this chapter we gain a glimpse of the common life in which we participate through the Spirit. John begins the chapter by an affirmation regarding the living Word, that is, the Word of life. He asserts that this Word was manifested, or embodied, and that the apostles had visual, audible, and manual proof of His existence upon the earth. They had heard Him, seen Him, and touched Him.

The life of the Word was eternal life, and when the apostles gazed upon the Son of God they saw eternal life incarnated. "We have seen it, and bear witness, and shew unto you that eternal life, which was with the Father, and was manifested unto us" (1 John 1:2; KJV). Three actions are referred to in this statement. The first was personal experience, and experience of the best kind. "We have seen." This provides eyewitness testimony. The second is public proclamation of the testimony, bearing witness to the world. The third is declaration to the saints for their edification and comfort. That which was manifested to the apostles was life, and that which they proclaimed to the saints was life. But it was not simply existence, it was life that had been with the Father, the God-life now shared with men in a bodily manifestation. This is important because it demonstrates that Christ came in order to show that eternal life can dwell in man even now.

The next statement of the apostle is significant, and yet few catch the significance of it. "That which we have seen and heard declare we unto you, that ye also may have fellowship [koinonia] with us: and truly our fellowship is with the Father, and with his Son Jesus Christ" (v. 3). The use of the word "fellowship" obscures the real meaning to modern minds, although the first-century disciples would have understood it.

Paul is clearly saying that the eternal life with the Father has now been embodied in a Son. Those who were called as His envoys have been made shareholders in this eternal life. The purpose of their testimony was that those who heard might share in the same common life with them, since the life in which they participated was with the Father and the Son. The Spirit not only operates upon our hearts through the good news to bring us into the life-sharing relationship, but dwells in our hearts in order to maintain that life within us. Just as there is no physical life without the spirit of man, so there is no spiritual life without the Spirit of God. "The Spirit is life because of righteousness" (Romans 8:10; KJV). The activating principle of the Spirit of life in

Christ Jesus makes us free from the law of sin and death.

Much is involved in the phrase, "the Spirit of life in Christ Jesus." This frees us from condemnation, and liberates us fom fear, including even the fear of death. The life is in the Son. On this matter there can be no quibbling. "In Him was life; and the life was the light of men" (John 1:4). "I am the way, and the truth, and the life" (John 14:6). It follows, then, that one who has the Son has life, and this is exactly what we are taught (1 John 5:11, 12).

To share in the life of the Spirit is to participate in eternal life, a transcendent personal relationship with God and Christ. The one God, the one Lord, and the one Spirit join in bestowing upon us grace, love, and eternal life. No greater gifts could possibly be offered to men in the flesh. No greater responsibility could be ours than to cherish and use these gifts to the glory of the Father. No more beautiful expression or benediction could be employed in closing a letter than that in which Paul closes his epistle to the Corinthians.

In this chapter it was pointed out that the Holy Spirit is in constant association with the Father and the Son. While different functions are peculiar to each, there is a divine harmony apparent in their relationships. It is not essential to faith that we understand all of the intricate workings of God, or that we comprehend in its fulness the spiritual realm. We have the testimony of God, and upon the basis of that evidence, we accept the personality and divinity of the Spirit.

6

Where Is the Spirit?

We have arrived at that point in our study of the Holy Spirit where we can investigate His actions toward men and the effect of their attitudes upon those actions. Many questions arise in the minds of those who seriously ponder these matters. How has the Spirit acted toward the unsaved to bring them into covenant relationship with God? Can such persons resist the Spirit, or are they plastic in His grasp, and changed without their own consent? What about His actions toward those who have been reconciled to God, delivered from the domain of darkness and translated into the kingdom of God's dear Son? Can they subdue and sublimate the Spirit, or render Him ineffective in their lives? In this last relationship we will learn that the Father has not abandoned us. We are not left simply to our own devices, but possess a divine Assistant, dwelling within our bodies and strengthening us in the warfare against evil. This is the basis of our hope.

When the apostle Paul was warning against immorality he predicated his solemn charge upon two grounds: the immoral man sins against his own body, and the Holy Spirit abides in that body. To sin against the body is to sin against the abode God has purchased and ordained for the Spirit. "Shun immorality. Every other sin which a man commits is outside the body; but the immoral man sins against his own body. Do you not know that your body is a temple of the Holy Spirit within you, which you have from God? You are not your own; you were bought with a price. So glorify God in your body" (1 Corinthians 6:18-20).

The Greeks had two words for "temple." Both are used in the Scriptures, but a distinction is made between them. *Hieron* designated the whole sacred enclosure and its precincts, including the outer courts, porches, and subordinate buildings. The other word *naos*, the one here employed, referred only to the Holy Place and Holy of Holies, the heart of the hallowed complex, and the dwelling-place of the Most High. Jesus taught inside the *hieron* in Jerusalem, but never entered the *naos*. Access to this was restricted to members of the priesthood, the tribe of Levi.

The only sanctuary God has on earth today is the consecrated human heart. He does not dwell in temples made with hands, and when men speak of material buildings as sanctuaries they use language that is not a part of the New Covenant concept. The heart of a man, like the heart of the temple, is the *naos* where God meets with him, and where the Spirit abides. It is interesting to remember that the word *hieron* is not once used metaphorically to designate the present dwelling of God. It is not the surroundings, but the heart, which is sanctified.

The temple of old in Jerusalem was erected as a place in which God's glory was manifested. During its dedication, "the house of the Lord, was filled with a cloud, so that the priests could not stand to minister because of the cloud; for the glory of the

Lord filled the house of God" (2 Chronicles 5:13, 14). That same glory floods the inner recesses of the bodies of the sanctified today, those who have been bought with a price, and they should glorify God in their bodies and spirits.

Under the first covenant, the worshiper had to go up to the house of the Lord. Now he is the house of the Lord. Then, each man had to take his offering to the priest, but now each man is a priest bringing an offering. Then, the Spirit was given to a select few to reveal God's will, now the Spirit is bestowed upon all those persons who have responded to that revelation.

That the Spirit sustains a personal relationship is indicated by the fact the He may be grieved. "And do not grieve the Holy Spirit of God, in whom you were sealed for the day of redemption" (Ephesians 4:30). Grief, a feeling or emotion, involves mental anguish, sorrow, or regret. That the Spirit can suffer from our offences or grieve because of our actions is proof of His personality. One cannot grieve a mere influence.

How can the Spirit be grieved? The context intimates that He may be offended by hurtful, vile, or filthy language. The preceding statement is, "Let no evil talk come out of your mouths, but only such as is good for edifying, as fits the occasion, that it may impart grace to those who hear" (v. 29). The succeeding statement shows we may grieve Him by our attitude toward the other saints. "Let all bitterness and wrath and anger and clamor and slander be put away from you, with all malice" (v. 31).

The Spirit dwells in every person who is a

member of the one body, and one member's speaking evil of or insulting another constitutes an assault upon the abode of the Spirit. In view of the anger, clamor, and slander, so prevalent in our day in communities of the saved, it is apparent that the Spirit must be often and deeply grieved. To employ filthy and obscene speech is to bring sadness to the Spirit, one of whose purposes in our lives is to cleanse and purify the inner temple.

In addition to one's grieving the Spirit, it is possible to lie to Him. This is evident in the case of Ananias and Sapphira, and is attested to by the apostle Peter. The original congregation of saints in Jerusalem included many widows within its fold. All of the members were Jews, among whom the synagogues always cared for their widows with special concern. A voluntary arrangement was introduced among the saints whereby those who wanted to could sell their real estate and chattels and deposit the receipts with the apostles. The apostles then purchased and distributed a daily allotment of food, paid for from the fund that was created under this agreement.

There was no compulsion to sell, and even those who did so were not obligated to bring the price and deliver it to the apostles. Ananias and his wife, perhaps motivated by a desire for praise, entered into a conspiracy. They would sell their land for a certain sum, retaining part of it for themselves while giving the remainder in such a way that it would create the impression it was the full amount (Acts 5:1-10). Ananias came into the place where the apostles were, only to be greeted by Peter with the question,

" 'Ananias, why has Satan filled your heart to lie to the Holy Spirit and to keep back part of the proceeds of the land?' " (Acts 5:3). He then informed the culprit that he had not lied to men, but to God. When he heard this accusation, Ananias dropped to the floor dead.

His wife, Sapphira, came in three hours later, not having been informed of the death of her husband. She was asked if the sum contributed was the full payment received for the land. She declared that it was, whereupon Peter asked, " 'How is it that you have agreed together to tempt the Spirit of the Lord?' " (Acts 5:9). Peter did not accuse them of lying about the Spirit, but to the Spirit. In so doing they tempted, or tried, the Spirit, and paid for it with their lives. If one can grieve, falsify to, and try the patience and knowledge of the Spirit, surely the Spirit is a divine personality.

The Holy Spirit can be resisted as He strives through the testimony revealed to men of God to bring the hearers into subjection to the divine will. This is clearly shown in the situation surrounding the death of Stephen, the first martyr to the Christian faith. The story is recorded in Acts 6 and 7. Stephen was a Hellenist, described as a man full of faith and the Holy Spirit. He did great wonders and miracles in Jerusalem in confirmation of his message concerning the Messiah. His effectiveness in making converts aroused the bitter ire of other foreign-born Jews living in the city and maintaining their synagogues. Their public disputes with him ended in a debacle for their cause and served only to impress the hearers with his wisdom and power. Unable to vanquish him in a debate, they resorted to other means, hiring men to accuse him of blasphemy against Moses and God. This crime was punishable by death, until Rome removed the right to execute from Palestinian nationals. In the tension then existing, however, a mob was formed, which surrounded and captured Stephen and hustled him away to the place where the Sanhedrin met, under the presidency of the high priest. False witnesses were paid to make accusation to the effect that they had heard him constantly blaspheme the holy city and the law. In support of this it was alleged that Stephen had distinctly announced more than once that Jesus of Nazareth would destroy the place and alter the law Moses had given. In accordance with the legal procedure of the council, the high priest asked the accused man, "Are these allegations true?"

Stephen made a masterful speech in defense. In reply to the first charge he affirmed that wherever God met with man it was a holy place, in proof of which he cited numerous cases to show that the greatest events in Jewish history took place outside of Palestine and Jerusalem. God appeared to Abraham in Chaldea, and to Joseph in Egypt. He called Moses at the burning bush in Midian, and distinctly told him to remove his shoes because the place was holy ground. The law itself was given at Sinai in the wilderness, not in Jerusalem.

Stephen further reminded them that when Solomon dedicated the temple he declared, "Yet the Most High does not dwell in houses made with hands" (Acts 7:48). The Lord had asserted, "Heaven is my throne, and earth my footstool" (v. 49). So the universe was hallowed, and one spot was no more sacred than another except as the lives of men made it so.

In answering the charge that he had blasphemed the law, Stephen recalled that even while Moses was up in the mount to receive the law, their fathers made a calf and offered sacrifices to it, rejoicing in the works of their hands (v. 41). He accused those present of receiving a law by the disposition of angels which they had never kept and were even then disobeying.

The climax of the address was reached in the impassioned words, " 'You stiffnecked people, uncircumcised in heart and ears, you always resist the Holy Spirit. As your fathers did, so do you' " (Acts 7:51). To enforce the truth of this charge he demanded that they name one prophet who had not been persecuted by their ancestors. He declared that the fathers had killed those who had predicted the coming of the Messiah, and the very ones now sitting before him had betrayed and murdered that Messiah when He came.

The sequel is well known. Members of what ordinarily was a stately gathering completely lost their composure. Screaming to drown out any further words from the speaker, and placing their hands over their ears, they converged upon him to silence him. Shoving him along, they hastened him outside the city limits, and, temporarily forgetting the ban on killing imposed by their Roman overlords, they stoned him to death.

It is apparent that stubborn disregard for the words spoken by the ambassadors of the Spirit constitutes resistance to the Spirit. This was true in ancient times when God's men spoke as the Holy Spirit motivated them. "In many and various ways God spoke of old to our fathers by the prophets" (Hebrews 1:1). This same God had also revealed to his "holy apostles and prophets" the mystery of Christ (Ephesians 3:5). To resist this message with unconsecrated heart and ears is to resist the Holy Spirit.

Some students of the Scriptures have suggested that the book we call "Acts of the Apostles" should have been named "Acts of the Holy Spirit." True, it does not contain all the acts of all the apostles, nor even all the acts of some of the apostles. It does record some of the acts of some of the apostles, but these men acted under the guidance and supervision of the Spirit. The direct assistance of the Spirit was not limited to the twelve. A good example is the case of Philip. He was one of the seven selected to relieve the apostles of daily distributing food to the many widows in the community of saints in Jerusalem. When violent persecution broke out against the church after the death of Stephen, it became necessary for the disciples to flee for safety to the country districts of Judea and Samaria, where they proclaimed with zeal the good news.

Philip entered into one of the cities of Samaria and announced the news of the Messiah with such accompanying demonstrations of power that the crowds listened eagerly to what Philip said, and there was great joy in that city (Acts 8:5-8). Under normal human arrangements Philip would have remained there to consolidate his remarkable success, but God had other plans for him.

Accordingly, the angel of the Lord instructed Philip to leave the city and travel southward to the road that led from Jerusalem toward Gaza. This former Philistine stronghold had long since been deserted. When he arrived at the highway junction, Philip caught sight of an Ethiopian reading from a scroll while riding in his chariot. At this point the Holy Spirit entered the picture by instructing Philip to "Go and join this chariot." Philip did so, and was used of the Spirit to clarify Scriptural matters that the Ethiopian government official did not understand.

When the man was satisfied that Jesus was the Messiah of whom the prophets had spoken, he asked what was to prevent him from being baptized. He ordered the chariot to stop, the two of them went down into the water, and Philip baptized him. The record is explicit at this point. "When they came up out of the water, the Spirit of the Lord caught up Philip; and the eunuch saw him no more" (Acts 8:39). One cannot help wondering about the reaction of the man when his recent companion disappeared, but he recovered and went happily on his way.

This indicates that the Spirit, who knows the hearts of men, operated to bring together one who knew the message and the other who needed it, was ready for it, and was honest enough to accept it. When the task was accomplished in a certain place or with a certain person, the messenger was removed. Philip, snatched away suddenly from the presence of the Ethiopian royal treasurer, appeared next in Azotus, passing through and preaching in all the cities until he reached Caesarea (Acts 8:40).

An even more interesting account of the direct activity of the Spirit in bringing together one who knew the good news and those who were eager to hear it is recorded in Acts 10. One cannot fully appreciate this account unless he remembers that until this time the good news has been shared with Jews and proselytes only. Even the Samaritans, although they were generally despised by the orthodox Jews, were circumcised, and they revered the Pentateuch, the writings of Moses.

Now the time had come to fulfill the divine goal of uniting Jews and Gentiles in one body through the Spirit. The first non-Jew chosen was Cornelius, a Roman centurion in the Italian cohort. We are told that Cornelius was a religious man, acknowledged as good and just by the whole Jewish nation (Acts 10:22). The Jew chosen to take the message was Simon Peter, a strict adherent of kosher regulations throughout his life.

After thorough investigation of the details, the story is exceptionally interesting. Cornelius, stationed at Caesarea, the headquarters for the Roman occupational forces, prayed regularly. One afternoon, while engaged in private devotions, he saw an angel who informed him that his prayers and acts of charity were recognized by God. He was told to send to Joppa for a man named Simon, who was also called Peter.

As soon as the angel vanished, Cornelius began to carry out the order. He summoned two household servants and a military orderly and sent them to Joppa to bring Peter back with them.

At noontime the next day, while the three men

were entering the city, Peter went up on the roof to pray. He became hungry, and while the household staff was preparing food he fell into a trance. In these words Luke describes what Peter envisioned: He saw "heaven opened, and something descending, like a great sheet, let down by four corners upon the earth. In it were all kinds of animals and reptiles and birds of the air. And there came a voice to him, 'Rise, Peter; kill and eat.' But Peter said, 'No, Lord; for I have never eaten anything that is common or unclean'" (Acts 10:11-14).

The voice came twice more and Peter made the same protest. Then the whole thing was taken up again into the sky. Immediately Peter came out of the trance, bewildered about the implications of the vision. At this very time, the three messengers, who had been inquiring about the location of the house, came to the front entrance and called out to ask if Simon Peter was there. The Holy Spirit told Peter to arise from where he was sitting and trying to figure out the vision, and go down to the ground floor. He further told Peter to accompany the three men who were asking for him, and to go without reluctance. He said, "I have sent them." In this instance the Spirit specifically sent messengers to locate a man with the message, then dispatched him with the messengers.

This did not end the direct involvement of the Spirit in the case of Cornelius. When Peter arrived at the home of Cornelius, he found relatives and friends of Cornelius awaiting him. After proper introduction Peter began to speak to them and now Peter recognized the meaning of the vision on the housetop. He knew now that it indicated that God was no respecter of persons, that national and ethnic differences no longer had any relevance. As Peter began to speak about Jesus of Nazareth, and reached the point where he said, "Whosoever believeth in him shall receive remission of sins" (v. 43; KJV), the Holy Spirit fell upon all those who heard.

Peter brought with him six Jewish brethren, who were utterly astonished when they heard the Gentiles begin to speak in tongues and to praise and glorify God. They realized that the Holy Spirit had been present and poured out upon the Gentiles as a gift. Peter asked, "Can any man forbid water, that these should not be baptized, which have received the Holy Ghost as well as we?" (v. 47; KJV). He commanded them to be baptized in the name of the Lord. Henceforth, there would be one body, composed of both Jews and Gentiles.

It is indicated by what we have thus far studied that the Spirit personally directed how and when men should act in the formative stage of the community of the redeemed. He sometimes directed an envoy to contact one who was ready for the saving truth, and other occasions sent men to find a proclaimer of the good news. At other times He barred the way into certain localities for those who had planned to infiltrate those places with the message.

One example of this will suffice. When Paul and Silas traveled through Syria and Cilicia, strengthening the congregations, they crossed over the Taurus Range, into the plains of Asia Minor. It was their intent, having labored in Phrygia and Galatia, to enter the province designated as Asia, but Luke records that they were forbidden by the Holy Spirit to do so (Acts 16:6). In view of this they skirted the area and started northward expecting to go into Bithynia, a region where a number of Diasporan Jews were to be found. Again they were thwarted because the Holy Spirit would not permit them to enter (Acts 16:7).

We can only surmise the reason for the circumvention of these plans. We do know that they came to Troas, where Paul had a vision in which a European citizen appeared and asked him to come into Macedonia and help them. A new continent was thus opened to the apostolic proclamation. The whole Grecian peninsula heard the message, and men and women rejoiced in the hope of the knowledge of Christ Jesus.

While we are thinking in terms of the action of the Spirit and the result of the attitudes of people toward such action, we should give attention to two other matters: quenching and blaspheming the Spirit. The second of these is in a category requiring special attention and will be reserved for the next chapter. We will conclude this segment of our study with a few observations about quenching the Holy Spirit.

The pointed admonition, "Do not quench the Spirit," occurs in 1 Thessalonians 5:19. The context may indicate that it relates to an attempt to restrain or inhibit those who possess special gifts of the Spirit. It may likewise refer to quelling the Spirit within oneself, not allowing Him free rein or control. The statement occurs just before another in the same vein which says, "Despise not prophesyings."

Prophecy was one of the special gifts mentioned in 1 Corinthians 12:10.

The word "quench" is ordinarily employed to signify smothering or extinguishing a fire. It is an appropriate term in view of the fact that the Spirit is sometimes spoken of as a flame or fire, and, paradoxically, as water. Thus the Spirit may be both kindled and poured out, depending upon the metaphor used at the time. A good example is found in 2 Timothy 1:6 where the young evangelist is told to stir up the gift of God which he possessed. The verb, in common use in the days of Paul, meant to rekindle, or renew a blaze, by poking and rearranging coals.

A fire may be quenched by any one of several methods. One may pour water upon it until it turns into dead coals and no longer flames up. Few of us need to be reminded of the occasions when we have seen someone, with intensity of purpose and zeal, completely squelched by constant rejection of his ideas and proposals. Many young Christians, and not a few older ones, have been driven to indifference by the constant reminder, "It will not work."

Again, a fire may be quenched by smothering it with noncombustible materials. In the parable of the sower, Jesus speaks of the seed falling among thorns. The quality of the seed was as high as that upon good ground, but the problem was that the thorns sprang up and choked it. The thorns are identified as the anxieties and pressures of the age in which we live, the deceitfulness of riches, and the lust of other things. It has often been assumed that the thicket of briers represented what is sometimes referred to as "the pleasures of life." It is true that one may become obsessed with recreation and sports, and we even use the word "fan," which is an abbreviation for fanatic, to describe such a person. But Jesus did not have this in mind at all.

Many of His hearers were hard pressed to survive in a land occupied by their Roman military masters. Few indeed had time to play or indulge in idle pastime. The "cares of this world" refer to the over-anxiety for food and clothing, and for the security mistakenly thought to reside in things. A subtile form of doubt besets those who think they have faith, when their faith is a trust in their own power and ability to become a success by piling up treasures on earth. Jesus condemned this lack of real faith. Nothing else tends to stifle the Spirit in one's life as does the attitude of those who would be rich in this world's goods.

A third way to quench a fire is simply to neglect it. One does not expect a fireplace to flame up, glow, and send forth heat from the fuel supplied it a week ago. There must be constant replenishment or else the fire will go out. One of the chief causes of failure is the "neglect of so great salvation," as the writer of Hebrews refers to it. Unless we regularly read the Word of God and pray, we will fail to survive. Yesterday's worship is like yesterday's warmth. It was welcome and stimulating at the time, but it will not warm the heart today.

A man who had once been a faithful follower of Jesus, but who had lapsed into unconcern and indifference, said, "I did not really deny the faith. I simply allowed it to slip away from me." The Badlands National Monument is an example of what can happen through erosion. Gradually through the centuries, land that once sustained an abundance of animal life by its growth in rich topsoil, began to erode until now it is a startling monument of waste and unproductiveness. So it is with many lives that once strengthened others, but are now badlands of apathy and ungodliness.

To quench the Spirit is to allow the purpose and meaning of life to burn low within. The personality becomes cold and hardened, and only the ashes remain to remind the world of a once warm spiritual being.

7

What Is the Sin Against the Spirit?

A perennial question for all who speak about the Holy Spirit is that of blasphemy, or sin against the Holy Spirit. The words of Jesus concerning all kinds of transgressions have been picked to pieces in order to identify what is popularly referred to as "the unpardonable sin." The result is that modern radio preachers have come up with a number of different "sins" to which this designation is applied. It is obvious they cannot all be correct, and it is possible none of them are. The consistent listener might almost be led to think the unforgiveable sin is one's failure to send a contribution to the preachers.

When Jesus used the expression, "blasphemy against the Spirit," He did so in contrast with "every sin and blasphemy." His words were, " 'Every sin and blasphemy will be forgiven men, but the blasphemy against the Spirit will not be forgiven' " (Matthew 12:31). Blasphemy is a specific sin against the Spirit as contrasted with every other sin. Integrity in interpretation demands that this fact govern any attempt at exegesis.

A widely-read expositor once took the indefensible position that deliberate murder of a Christian constituted the sin against the Holy Spirit. He reasoned that the body of such a person was the temple of the Holy Spirit. The man made out an elaborate case and arranged a quantity of Scriptures in defense of his position, but several things are wrong with it. Blasphemy has nothing to do with an act of murder. Furthermore, murder can be forgiven, and was, even when perpetrated against the only begotten Son of God. On the cross Jesus prayed for those who were taking His life: " 'Father, forgive them; for they know not what they do' " (Luke 23:34). If their sin was unforgiveable, such a prayer would have been a farce. The fact is, the prayer was answered a little more than seven weeks later, on the Day of Pentecost, in the city of Jerusalem. Peter confronted the Jews who were present, saying, "This Jesus, who did many miracles and wonders among you, you crucified and killed through lawless and merciless men" (Acts 2:22, 23). Yet, when those who heard this were stabbed by their consciences and asked what they must do, Peter replied, " 'Repent, and be baptized every one of you in the name of Jesus Christ for the forgiveness of your sins; and you shall receive the gift of the Holy Spirit' " (v. 38). The prayer of Jesus for the forgiveness of His murderers was answered when the sinners complied with the terms of forgiveness as laid down by the Father.

A preacher, who had sought without success to counsel a person of suicidal tendencies, wrote a booklet advancing the idea that suicide was the unpardonable sin. His reasoning was that the sin was premeditated, and in the commission of it the sinner cut off all opportunities for repentance. For that reason he placed himself outside the pale of forgiveness. But this is certainly not the sin about which Jesus was speaking. If suicide is an unpardonable sin, there are two such sins, rather than just one.

Suicide is the taking of human life, but the degree of culpability for the act will have to be assessed by God who knows the hearts of men. Certainly the perpetrator, who is also the victim, cannot be judged by a human tribunal, although men are prone to make posthumous statements about such situations. Only God can know the mental state at the time when one takes his life. There is no ground for saying a person who commits suicide cannot be forgiven. He may be, but if this is so, it will not be because of the impossibility of forgiveness due to the nature of the act.

Perhaps the most common of all the opinions about one's sinning against the Spirit is that it is resistance against the call of the Spirit until death overtakes the sinner. There is a fallacy in this kind of rationalization, however. Certainly the Spirit operates upon the heart of the sinner through the message proclaimed, but there is a difference between resisting and blaspheming. While it is dangerous indeed to reject an appeal to commit one's life to the lordship of Jesus, the sin is not unforgiveable, but unforgiven. If it were unforgiveable, each person would be afforded but one opportunity to obey the gospel, and if he refused, he could never be forgiven. One who stubbornly persists in rejecting the call of God's grace will die in an unforgiven state because he dies in his sins. But his sins and stubbornness could have been forgiven at any time.

Blasphemy against the Spirit is not forgiveable. It is unique, and its uniqueness lies in its nature and the object of the blasphemy. Why, then, do men ascribe so many and divergent actions to it? The answer is simple. They lift a statement out of its setting and, by isolating it from its Scriptural background, they can arbitrarily make it mean anything that seems rational to themselves. This is responsible for most of the misunderstanding in the religious realm.

None of the words of Jesus were spoken in a vacuum. None of His acts were performed by accident. Every passage of Scripture was originally given in a three-fold context of time (history), place (geography), and revelation. To ignore this context is to handle the Word of God unfairly and to reach unwarranted and unjustifiable conclusions. Let us consider what has become a thorny problem in exegesis from the Scriptural framework in which it appears.

At the time Jesus made the statement regarding the sin against the Holy Spirit, He was at the peak of His acclaim by the masses. "A great multitude from Galilee followed him, and from Judaea, and from Jerusalem, and from Idumaea, and from beyond Jordan; and they about Tyre and Sidon, a great multitude, when they had heard what great things he did, came unto him" (Mark 3:7, 8; KJV). He told the disciples to keep a boat ready, to prevent His being crushed by the crowd. The record says, "For he had healed many; insomuch that they pressed upon him for to touch him, as many as had plagues" (v. 10). Mark especially refers to the fact that when He confronted those who were possessed by demons, the evil spirits would fall at His feet and cry aloud, "You are the Son of God."

All of this had a profound impact upon the common people and they refused to be dismissed. They surged around Jesus, wondering about and discussing His claims. When Jesus entered a house, the crowd pressed in until it was impossible for the disciples to eat. To add to the general excitement, a rumor was conveyed to Nazareth that Jesus had lost His mental faculties and was acting like a crazed person. "When his friends heard of it, they went out to lay hold on him: for they said, He is beside himself" (v. 21).

Among the more interested observers of this growing influence were the Pharisees and Sadducees. Their motives for trying to check it were different, however. The Sadducees were political opportunists, compromising with Rome and seeking to curb any movement that might develop into a revolution. Such would bring down swift punishment by the Roman legions, with a consequent loss of official positions, which were always tenuous in an occupied territory.

The Pharisees were the watchdogs of orthodoxy. Their concern was that the rabble (as they regarded the people) should not be led away from the body of rabbinical tradition by which their every move in life was regulated. Jesus was attached to no sect. He was neither Pharisee, Sadducee, nor Essene. He was not a product of any rabbinical school. He was from Nazareth, a despicable city away from the great centers of learning and culture. As the Pharisees saw Him, He was a mere carpenter, a descendant of peasant stock, and a rabble-rousing miracle worker. Their chief concern was to keep Him from securing too large a following. They were willing to go to any lengths to do this. They knew the superstition and fears of the masses. Many of these no doubt resulted from an unwholesome mixture of Chaldean and Persian ideas (acquired during the exile) and legendary traditions of the rabbis.

It would hardly serve our immediate purpose to detail the often absurd fears of the people in the days of our Lord upon the earth. The *Shedim*, or evil spirits, lurked ever near, occupying the atmosphere, awaiting the moment to plague the unfaithful and forgetful. Whether the term *Shedim* is from a primitive root meaning "to fly about" or "to rebel" is now a question, but in those days men were never free from the concern that an evil spirit might move in upon them at any moment. The rabbis cautioned against certain things considered to be especially dangerous because of demons. It was unwise to walk between two palm trees growing more than six feet apart. It was improvident to borrow drinking water from a passerby, or to walk over water that had been poured out, or spilled upon the ground. The last danger could be averted by sprinkling dust upon the earth, or removing one's shoes and walking through barefoot.

Now we must give attention to another word with which our analysis must reckon: *Beelzebul*. There is no doubt that this is the correct term, rather than *Beelzebub*, for every passage of the New Covenant Scriptures in which it appears. It is probable that early translators sought to accommodate it to the Philistine term for the god of flies. Because of a somewhat kindred word in Hebrew, which means "to fertilize land with dung," some scholars have assumed that Beelzebul was "lord of dung," or, ruler of the unclean. Alfred Edersheim, the Jewish scholar, has pointed out that Zibbul actually means sacrificing to idols. Beelzebul would therefore be the same as lord or chief of idolatrous sacrificing, the worst and chief of all demons, presiding over and inciting to idolatry. Idolatry was specifically forbidden by the first two Commandments of the Decalogue. To seduce to idolatry or false worship was regarded as the ultimate in disrespect for God. To accuse one of operating by the authority or under the power of Beelzebul was to league him with the very spirit of malevolence, as opposed to all righteousness and moral goodness.

With this bit of background of the circumstances under which Jesus operated, we are ready to investigate the events that called forth His denunciation of those who blasphemed against the Holy Spirit. For the purpose bringing consistency into the interpretation, enabling one to check the Scriptural language, the discussion will be limited mainly to the language of the *Revised Standard Version*. Other renderings are used, if they make for greater clarity.

The argument is centered primarily around the accounts found in Matthew 12:22-32 and Mark 3:22-30. I am assuming that these two passages cover the same incident and speech. Those who disagree will grant that my dealing with the text itself, which is the present concern, will be fair.

The incident began when a blind and dumb demonic was brought to Jesus. Jesus healed the man in the presence of the people, who attested that the demoniac both spoke and saw. This kind of sign could not be denied, and it created astonishment in the hearts of the beholders. In their amazement they began to ask one another, " 'Can this be the Son of

David?' '' (Matthew 12:23). Because of this, the Pharisees, jealous for themselves and the law, said, " 'It is only by Beelzebul, the prince of demons, that this man casts out demons' '' (v. 24). They could not deny that a miracle had occurred, but they could belittle it. It is obvious that they were not true to their own convictions, but spoke these words to keep the superstitious people from following Jesus. One of their own number, who was a ruler among them, had come to Jesus after dark, and confessed, " 'Rabbi, we know that you are a teacher come from God; for no one can do these signs that you do, unless God is with him' '' (John 3:2). The Pharisees knew that Jesus was not in league with the prince of demons. This was a ruse intended to counteract the influence of the Son of God with the common people.

Jesus demonstrated the absurdity of their accusation by three arguments. The first showed the folly of a power that would be antagonistic against itself. He said, " 'Every kingdom divided against itself is laid waste, and no city or house divided against itself will stand; and if Satan casts out Satan, he is divided against himself; how then will his kingdom stand?' '' (Matthew 12:25, 26). One can but imagine the chagrin of the lawyers when this fallacy was pointed out to them publicly.

The second argument dealt with the inconsistency manifested in claiming that Jesus operated under the authority of Beelzebul in expelling demons, while students of the Pharisaic school also claimed to cast them out. The word "sons" here is employed for disciples or students. For example, the "sons" of the prophets were students of the

110

prophets, who sought to learn from and imitate them.

In Judaism of that day, many teachings existed about the exorcising of evil spirits. Many persons believed that pronunciation of the "ineffable name" of God would drive demons forth, and there were various combinations of terms to be recited to put the *Shedim* to flight. Jesus did not enter into a debate as to the legitimacy of the claims of the disciples of the Pharisees. It was the contention of the Pharisees that their students could drive out demons, so the question was, if it required authority from the prince of demons to do so, were they operating in league with demons also. Jesus said, " 'They shall be your judges' " (v. 27).

On the other hand, to admit that the Spirit of God drove out the demons was to admit that the kingdom of God had come upon them. The Jews believed a kingdom of darkness was presided over by the prince of demons. If Jesus had been operating under the authority of that prince, the kingdom of darkness was predominant, but if He manifested the Spirit of God, the rule of Heaven was triumphing over Satan, laying his kingdom waste.

The third argument had to do with the relative strength required to subdue a man before plundering his house and dispossessing him. " 'Or how can one enter a strong man's house and plunder his goods, unless he first binds the strong man? Then indeed he may plunder his house' " (v. 29). In this example the strong man is Satan. His goods are represented by the demons infesting the bodies of unfortunate victims, such as the one who had been afflicted by

111

blindness and loss of speech. The argument of Jesu
is clear. Before He could cast out demons He woul
have needed to subdue Satan and gain control of hi
holdings and property. Satan would no more sur
render his stronghold than a man would willingly le
a marauder come upon his premises and throw hi
possessions into the street. The observers' admissio
that Jesus was driving out demons was also an ad
mission that He had gained superiority over Satan.

These arguments presented a real dilemma t
the Pharisees. If Jesus operated under the power o
Beelzebul, Satan was fighting against his own forces
and his kingdom would disintegrate. If not, Jesu
had entered in, bound Satan, and was despoiling hi
kingdom. The kingdom of Satan was doomed an
the superiority of Jesus was admitted, regardless o
which position His opposers assumed.

At this point, Jesus inserted a rather peculia
statement, according to Matthew. Its relevance is no
seen at first glance. Jesus said, " 'He who is not wit
me is against me, and he who does not gather wit
me scatters' " (v. 30). A little thought will reveal tha
He was pointing out that there are but two kingdom
in the universe, by nature hostile toward each other
There was no cessation of warfare between them
and no compromise. The Son of God and the son o
perdition had nothing in common. There was n
concord between Christ and Belial, as Paul phrases i
in 2 Corinthians 6:15. Jesus had nothing to do wit
demons, or with the prince of demons, except to de
feat their every intent and purpose.

We are now ready for the statement relating t
the sin of blaspheming against the Holy Spirit

" 'Therefore I tell you, every sin and blasphemy will be forgiven men, but the blasphemy against the Spirit will not be forgiven. And whoever says a word against the Son of man will be forgiven; but whoever speaks against the Holy Spirit will not be forgiven, either in this age or in the age to come' " (Matthew 12:31, 32).

Without speaking it is impossible to commit the sin of blasphemy. Blasphemy is a sin of the tongue and not merely of the heart. Regardless of how wrong one may be in his thinking, blasphemy must be openly expressed. Our word "blasphemy" is not a translation. It is a transliteration of the Greek original which means "to speak reproachfully, to slander, calumniate, rail at, or revile." To blaspheme is to speak injuriously of that which is high or holy. Blasphemy is never justifiable, but it is forgiveable upon proper repentance when directed against any other person or thing than the Holy Spirit. This is so, even if it involved Jesus. " 'Whoever says a word against the Son of man will be forgiven' " (v. 32).

What is the unforgiveable sin? According to the context, it is accrediting to Satan the power by which Jesus performed His wonderful works. It is saying that Jesus possessed an evil spirit rather than the Holy Spirit. This is made quite clear by Mark, who writes that Jesus uttered His warning about blasphemy against the Spirit, "For they had said, 'He has an unclean spirit' " (Mark 3:30). There may be more to the matter than a mere statement, however, for the motivation must not be forgotten.

If those who saw Jesus perform His wonderful works had actually believed, sincerely, that He was using the power of Satan to dislodge demons, they would not have been guilty of blaspheming against the Holy Spirit. Their verbal conclusion would not have constituted this sin. They would have been sadly mistaken and the conclusion would have been irrational; yet, with increasing knowledge they could have changed their minds and obtained forgiveness for their error.

The blasphemy against the Spirit is to deliberately attribute to Satan the power by which Jesus performed His miracles, against all evidence and for the purpose of deflecting the hearts of humble men and women from faith in Him. The utterance of the slander is simply the result of a malevolent heart, conspiring to defeat the very purpose for which Jesus came in the flesh. It is a willful decision to scatter what He has come to gather, and the statement is a lie born of the will to deceive. This raises several questions.

Why is this unprincipled calumniation of the Spirit so heinous? What places it in a category by itself as the only sin for which forgiveness is not provided? Why is it worse than every other sin and blasphemy, including speaking against the Son of man? A little reflection on the purpose of the Spirit in producing the miracles of Jesus may help to explain the matter.

In general, Jesus performed two kinds of works—intellectual and physical—to excite wonder and to produce faith in Him as the Messiah. The first consisted of predictions as to the future, and faith in this case was deferred until the event came to pass. When an occurrence transpired and the mind recalled that Jesus had previously predicted it exactly as it happened, faith was kindled in His claim to have divine prescience. " 'I tell you this now, before it takes place, that when it does take place you may believe that I am he' " (John 13:19).

Physical miracles were of the kind to incite immediate recognition of supernatural power. Thus the statement, "And when they saw these things, they believed" expresses the idea that the validation of the act was in its nature. It was visual, and the impact was immediate. Physical miracles had a twofold motivation, resulting from compassion for the suffering and the need for a criterion by which to establish the divinity of a mission. The relief of physical pain or infirmity was intended to provide an incentive to believe.

Belief in Jesus was not a mere exercise of consciousness, but a matter of life and death. He said to the Jews, " 'I told you that you would die in your sins, for you will die in your sins unless you believe that I am he' " (8:24). Jesus also appealed to His works as visual testimony to occasion faith: " 'But the testimony which I have is greater than that of John; for the works which the Father has granted me to accomplish, these very works which I am doing, bear me witness that the Father has sent me' " (5:36). Again, " 'If I am not doing the works of my Father, then do not believe me; but if I do them, even though you do not believe me, believe the works, that you may know and understand that the Father is in me and I am in the Father' " (10:37, 38).

John 20:30, 31 is pregnant with meaning: "Now Jesus did many other signs in the presence of the disciples, which are not written in this book; but these are written that you may believe that Jesus is the Christ, the Son of God, and that believing you may have life in his name." It is evident that the Spirit exercised selectivity in placing on record the various miracles of which we may read. Out of the great number of signs Jesus did, a sufficient number were selected to convince any honest heart that He was the Messiah and God's Son. A dishonest heart would not believe in Him regardless of the amount of proof produced.

The signs Jesus did by the Holy Spirit were designed to make believers in Him. A deliberate attempt to frustrate faith by false accusations as to the source of power would therefore be a sin of the deepest dye. It would amount to a malicious conspiracy to deprive men of eternal life because of personal jealousy and hostility. One might honestly question the claims of Jesus, and might verbalize doubts about the authenticity and genuineness of Jesus' words as recorded. This is not unforgiveable. Further research and study could well demonstrate one's error and bring about real reformation. To behold the signs done to produce faith, and against all observation, knowledge, and conscience, assign that power to Satan for the specific purpose of destroying faith is to condemn mankind once and for all to eternal death.

Why is there no forgiveness for this malign act? The simplest answer is that God has placed it outside the pale of divine forgiveness. It is beyond the limit set for grace. It is the one crime against divine majesty that is outside the circle. This does not exhaust the subject, however. The kind of heart that would engage in such reprehensible conduct will not repent. It is the heart of stone or flint that would willingly see the world of mankind destroyed to justify its own cruelty and gratify its own inhumanity.

The question always arises, "What if one in this condition should repent?" This need not trouble us. One who is dead to love for all truth, and has crucified in his consciousness all respect for evidence will not believe. Faith is the belief of testimony, and one who has examined the testimony and defiantly assigned it to the realm of the damned has no ground left for honest faith. He has sinned away his day of grace!

Can men commit the unpardonable sin today? The answer, I think, is that it is possible, but not very probable. That it is possible can be deduced from the words of Jesus, " 'Whoever speaks against the Holy Spirit will not be forgiven, either in this age or in the age to come' " (Matthew 12:32). Among the Jews who were present when these words were spoken, the expression "the age to come," referred to the Messianic age, the time when, according to their thinking, the Messiah would sit upon His throne and exercise universal dominion. There is no reason to believe that Jesus employed the term in any other than the accepted sense, just as there is no reason to think that He endorsed the traditional ideas with which the rabbis had invested it.

"This age" refers to the dispensation in which Jesus lived upon the earth. "The age to come" refers to the dispensation in which we now live. There would be little value in applying this latter expression to the age following the general resurrection from the dead, for no unforgiven sins will be forgiven then. It is my conviction that one can commit the sin in this age and if so, it is as unforgiveable now as it was when Jesus said it.

We should not allow the matter to rest here without making a few comments about an attempted current application of the remarks of Jesus. In our own time an interest has been aroused in the work of the Holy Spirit, with the result that many persons claim to have received special gifts of the Spirit, to enable them to perform signs and wonders. Radio stations specializing in "gospel broadcasting" have one program after another, from sunrise to sunset, in which men use their alleged gifts as drawing-cards to solicit contributions and plead for offerings to keep them on the air.

A frequent tactic with which to ward off any criticism and to stifle any protest is to threaten that those who question the sincerity of the speakers may be guilty of blaspheming against the Holy Spirit. There is no attempt here to enter into the controversy as to whether or not the "charismatic gifts" are for this generation. That is a study that lies outside the scope of the volume. Honest doubts about the qualifications, objectives, and character of some of the "radio evangelists" is not sinning against the Spirit. By no stretch of the imagination can honest investigation of their claims be remotely connected to what Jesus said.

During my lifetime I have found certain individuals who were deeply troubled by the thought that they might have committed the sin against the

118

Holy Spirit, and were condemned to a state of hopelessness here and of condemnation hereafter. Without fail, I have found that the real trouble was ignorance of what Jesus was talking about. Frequently the problem resulted from misinformation derived from an overzealous exhorter who sought to frighten the person into a public response to his call. A simplistic, but relatively safe, criterion is that anyone who is worried about having blasphemed the Spirit has not done so, for the kind of person Jesus described would never worry about it.

I have canvassed rather extensively what I regard as the Scriptural teaching related to the blasphemy against the Spirit. It seems apparent that the sin does not refer to an attitude toward a mere influence, impersonal force or energy, but consists of the slander of a divine personality through which God's purpose is accomplished in the universe of His creation. Yet, if I stop the discussion here, at least two other passages will go unexplained. Many have equated these with the unforgiveable sin of which Jesus spoke. Having written at this length on the theme, it seems injudicious to ignore the other problem passages, so I will deal with them as peripheral questions, not specifically related to the central concern of this work, and yet deserving of scrutiny and attention.

APOSTASY

The first passage is found in Hebrews 6:4-8 and reads as follows: "For it is impossible to restore again to repentance those who have once been enlightened, who have tasted the heavenly gift, and have become partakers of the Holy Spirit, and have tasted the goodness of the word of God and the powers of the age to come, if they then commit apostasy, since they crucify the Son of God on their own account and hold him up to contempt. For land which has drunk the rain that often falls upon it, and brings forth vegetation useful to those for whose sake it is cultivated, receives a blessing from God. But if it bears thorns and thistles, it is worthless and near to being cursed; its end is to be burned.''

On the basis of the statement of the impossibility of restoring to repentance those who are in the category here described, thousands of persons think of apostasy as the unforgiveable sin. Again, the problem lies in ignoring the context. Scriptural context may be either immediate and direct, or remote. The first has to do with the setting adjacent to a statement, either preceding or following it, or both. The remote context has to do with the aim and purpose of a letter or section that governs the relationship of all that appears in the entire frame of reference.

A careful study of the entire Hebrew letter will reveal that it was written to Palestinian Jews, as the title indicates. It was written during a time when the temple was still standing in Jerusalem and the priests were daily ministering within its precincts. The addressees had accepted Jesus as the Messiah, but because of the appeal of the pomp and pageantry of the temple ritual, or because of persecution and opposition, were defecting to Judaism and abandoning the faith of the gospel. The whole purpose of this letter was to strengthen them to stand firm, ''For we share in Christ, if only we hold our first confidence firm to the end" (Hebrews 3:14).

The method of encouragement was to point out that in Christ we have something far better than was found under Moses and in the Old Covenant. The word "better" occurs thirteen times, and in each instance points up the superiority of some feature in Christ over what Judaism had to offer. It must be remembered that the first-century Jewish believer who forgot the Lord and returned to his previous relationship, discounted the value of the blood of Christ. He once again placed his trust in inferior animal sacrifices, the blood of bulls and goats, which could never take away sins (10:4).

There is a difference between one's "leaving the church" or "going back into the world," as the phraseology of our day often states it, and one's going back into dead works from which the conscience has been purified. Modern "drop-outs" frequently affirm that they believe in Jesus as much as they ever did, but, because of the weakness of the flesh, they cannot live up to the responsibility of being a Christian. The letter to the Hebrews was not addressed to individuals like this, but to those who have "spurned the Son of God, and profaned the blood of the covenant by which they were sanctified, and outraged the Spirit of grace" (10:29).

With this preliminary survey we are prepared to look at the passage under discussion. These Hebrews had once been enlightened, which in this instance refers to the illumination of God's purpose in Christ. "In him was life, and the life was the light of men" (John 1:4). They had left the moonlight age with its shadows, symbols, and types, and were translated into the sunlight dispensation of reality and fulfillment. The situation was like one's leaving a storm cellar lighted by a single flickering candle and coming into a house aglow with fluorescent lighting.

The Christians had "tasted the heavenly gift." The word "taste," as used in the Scriptures, does not mean simply to sample. The term means to experience or share in something. The "heavenly gift" does not refer to the Spirit, which is expressly mentioned in the following statement. It no doubt has to do with that quality of life gained through reception of the Lord Jesus Christ, Heaven's greatest gift to humanity.

They had "become partakers of the Holy Spirit." The promise of God to His people through the prophets was that He would grant them His Spirit to dwell in them. We discussed at length the assurance Jesus gave before His departure from earth that He would send another Helper. Accordingly, those who heard the word of truth, the gospel of salvation, and believed in Jesus, were said to be "sealed with the promised Holy Spirit" (Ephesians 1:13). Under the legal dispensation of Moses, the Spirit invested certain men with the gift of prophetic utterance, leaving the great body of people without direct association with the Spirit. In the gospel age the Spirit dwells in all who are in Christ, and the Hebrews who had been the first to hear the good news had been so blessed.

They had "tasted the goodness of the word of God." The gospel, a message of joy and hope, brought comfort to the sick and assurance to the dying. It did not require dead sacrifices nor enjoin the killing of animals. Rather, it emphasized the giving of the body of the believer as a living sacrifice, holy, acceptable to God, as a rational and understandable service. The contrast was vividly stated in one verse of the Hebrew letter. "For if the sprinkling of defiled persons with the blood of goats and bulls and with the ashes of a heifer sanctifies for the purification of the flesh, how much more shall the blood of Christ, who through the eternal Spirit offered himself without blemish to God, purify your conscience from dead works to serve the living God" (Hebrews 9:13, 14).

The Christians had experienced "the powers of the age to come" (Hebrews 6:5). Again, this refers to the Jewish concept of the Messianic age. The writer to the Hebrews regarded that age has having arrived. The Son of God was sitting at the right hand of the Father. Angels, archangels, authorities, and powers were made subject to Him. God had highly exalted Him and given Him a name above every name. He was made head of the community of the called-out ones. The "age to come" had arrived!

The writer declares that if those who have participated in all of these blessings should now "commit apostasy," it is impossible to restore them to repentance. The word rendered "apostasy" is from a term meaning to fall away. It refers to an abandonment of the faith, a denial of the validity of the facts upon which belief is founded, an utter desertion of the truth of the gospel. Such desertion is not the result of ignorance, but is a deliberate step taken with eyes wide open to the truth.

Those who fall away crucify the Son of God afresh and hold Him in contempt. How do they do this? The answer is simple. Jesus was condemned to be crucified because He testified that He was the Messiah. Those who lived upon earth in His day preferred their legalistic ritual with the earthly gifts and animal sacrifices. They considered Jesus a threat to their traditions. Men's forsaking Him and going back to the shadows of the law was like crucifying Jesus anew and making it appear that His death was empty and useless.

Defection from the faith under such circumstances gave the enemies of the cross an excuse for rejoicing and an opportunity for ridicule. It weakened the morale of the saints. The very name of Jesus became the butt of scurrilous remarks and was slandered in the eyes of the heathen populace.

Those who forsook Jesus to return to legalistic bondage were likened to cultivated land. A farm that drinks in the rain and repays the tillage of its fields with fruitful crops is blessed of God because of its abundant yield. Sterile or barren ground, or land that produces only a matted growth of thorns and thistles, is fit only for execration and will be burned over to destroy its noxious growth. This last is an apt picture of those who have received every blessing from Heaven, only to use the strength to disgrace and disparage the cause for which Jesus died.

Apostasy, as serious as it may be, is not the blasphemy against the Spirit. One may fall away without overtly slandering the Spirit. The record does not say that such a person cannot repent, rather that it is impossible for another to lead him to repentance. The reason is understood when we remember that every act is the result of motivation. The apostate has listened to and examined every motive leading to repentance. He has experienced every blessing and benefit accruing from relationship with Christ. When he turns his back upon all of these, no other appeal remains that can restore him.

We must retain a clear distinction between an apostate and an ordinary backslider. One may become a drop-out without renouncing Jesus. It is possible to become negligent and to forsake responsibility without denying the validity of the claims of God upon one's life, or the efficacy of the blood of Christ as a cleansing agent for sin. Expositors need to be careful that they do not discourage those who could resume the yoke of Christ by making it appear that they are in such a state they cannot do so.

THE SIN UNTO DEATH

Another passage that presents some real problems is 1 John 5:16, 17. Here John mentions the "sin unto death." *The Revised Standard Version* designates it a "mortal" sin. Many persons have concluded that this is the sin against the Holy Spirit, of which Jesus spoke. I do not believe the two are identical, and I shall briefly discuss why I do not.

"If any man see his brother sin a sin which is not unto death, he shall ask, and he shall give him life for them that sin not unto death. There is a sin unto death: I do not say that he shall pray for it. All unrighteousness is sin: and there is a sin not unto death" (KJV). In verse 15 John had given assurance that we will be heard in our petitions to God because of our faith in His Son. John then qualifies this by distinguishing between a "sin unto death" and one not "unto death." This has occasioned much conjecture upon the part of commentators. Many different views have been expressed. Albert Barnes regarded the "sin unto death" as the unpardonable sin. This view was also shared by Philip Doddridge. A lengthy dissent was registered to their view, however, by Dr. James Macknight in his *Apostolical Epistles*.

Dr. Macknight held that in the early age of Christianity, God punished some men for their sins directly with physical disease or infirmity, and in aggravated cases, with death. His position was that if someone in that age who was possessed of the gift of healing saw one smitten of God and could determine that the punishment of death was not assessed, he could pray for that person and God would honor the gift by granting life to the one so smitten.

There can be little doubt that God punished certain sins with death. This was true in the case of Ananias and Sapphira, who conspired together to lie about the amount of money they received for the sale of their property (Acts 5:1-10). It is also true that, because of irregularities in observation of the Lord's Supper, some at Corinth were smitten with sickness and others suffered death (1 Corinthians 11:30). Here Paul declares that those who eat and drink with the wrong motive, eat and drink punishment to themselves. He added, "For this cause many are weak and sickly among you, and many sleep." Here is the full text of Dr. Macknight's treatment of the passage under consideration:

"Because it was necessary to the successful propagation of the gospel, that its professors in the first age should be remarkably holy, God so ordered it that the open miscarriages of individuals, were often punished with visible temporal judgments. So Paul told the Corinthians, who had been guilty of great irregularities in the celebration of the Lord's Supper, 1 Corinthians 11:30, 'For this cause many of you are sick, and some of you are dead.' These judgments, being public, had no doubt a great influence in restraining the first Corinthians from sin. On the other hand to encourage those to repent who by their sins had brought on themselves mortal diseases, there were in the first age, persons, who being endowed with the gift of healing diseases miraculously, (1 Corinthians 12:9), were moved by the Holy Ghost to heal the sick, who had repented of the sins which had brought on them the diseases under which they were laboring. We may therefore believe, that when John directed *any one*, who saw his brother sinning a sin not unto death, to ask God to give him life, he did not mean any ordinary Christian, but any spiritual man who was endowed with the gift of healing diseases; and that the brother for whom the spiritual man was to ask life, was not every brother who had sinned, but the brother only who had been punished for his sin with some mortal disease, but who having repented of his sin, it was not a sin unto death: and that the life to be asked for such a brother was not eternal life, but a miraculous recovery from the mortal disease under which he was laboring."[9]

W. E. Vine concurs in the view expressed by Macknight. In his book, *The Epistles of John*, he writes as follows:

[9]James Macknight, D.D., *Apostolical Epistles* (Philadelphia: Thomas Wardle, 1841), pp. 673, 674.

"The phrase 'unto death' signifies 'tending towards death,' rather than the actual condition of being in death. Accordingly, this would seem to rule out the view that the state referred to is that in which a child of God has lost all communion with the Lord, for that would involve a condition of spiritual death, already experienced, instead of that which tends toward it.

"As to the subject of death, the only conclusion that seems possible is that the reference is to physical death. That is spoken of as the result of certain sins, as in the case of Ananias and Sapphira, and that of the moral delinquent in 1 Corinthians 5, and again in the case of those who partake of the Lord's Supper unworthily (1 Corinthians 11:30), where sleep refers to physical death."[10]

To me this seems to harmonize best with the circumstances and with the Scriptures. If God visited sickness upon a brother because he had sinned, and another had the power of discernment by which he could determine that the divine decree did not involve death as a part of the punishment, he could pray for the sick man and life would be granted to the man as a result of the petition. He would not have to continue in his punishment. "The prayer of faith will save the sick man, and the Lord will raise him up; and if he has committed sins, he will be forgiven" (James 5:15).

On the other hand, if the sin was such that God decreed death, or capital punishment, prayer would be unavailing. "There is a sin unto death: I do not say

---

[10]First printed by Oliphants, Ltd., England. Published in Britain without copyright.

that he shall pray for it" (1 John 5:16; KJV). Of course, it would have been useless for Peter to have prayed for Ananias and Sapphira. Three hours after Ananias died for his guilt, Peter told Sapphira she would suffer the same fate because she was equally involved in the sin. God has no double standard.

I do not think the record means to imply that there was a specific sin "unto death," any more than there was a specific sin "not unto death." The difference lay, not in the overt act, but in the motivation and nature of the one committing the sin. Ananias and Sapphira died because of a lie growing out of a conspiracy. The Corinthians died because of their partisan debasement of the Lord's Supper. Many commentators think that "the destruction of the flesh" referred to in the case of the blatant fornicator (1 Corinthians 5:5) meant a death decree when he was turned over to Satan.

Does God still directly visit sickness and death upon men and women who are guilty of kindred sins? Although my answer will not satisfy everyone who reads this book, I am not hesitant to say I do not believe that He does. In the primitive era of the community of the called-out ones, a directness of dealing was essential. This directness is not now essential to the fulfillment of the divine purpose. At that time there were no New Covenant Scriptures to circulate as guidelines for spiritual and moral behavior, nor to remind men that they would be "reserved unto the judgment of that great day."

Every social institution requires certain measures in its inception and foundational era, that it may later outgrow or discard. Kingdoms and nations mature as do the individuals who compose them. As succeeding generations develop an increasing sense of responsibility, methods of punishing derelictions of duty may change. "Jesus Christ is the same yesterday, today, and forever" does not mean God limits His methods today to what He did in previous centuries. He is no longer obligated to relieve the hunger of five thousand persons with five loaves and two fish. Neither should we think Him obligated to grant men and women the same gifts as He did in the formative stages of the church. Indeed, this is one sign that few "miracle workers" lay claim to performing, although it would be a tremendous asset to missionaries in famine-stricken areas.

I do not consider the sin "unto death" as being the blasphemy against the Spirit. I cannot conceive of the sin against the Spirit as being a reflection against, or a rejection of, a mere influence in the world. The Scriptures seem to indicate that blasphemy is an assault upon and a false accusation of a divine Person, so grave in nature as to place the one who commits it outside the domain of God's forgiveness.

8

What Is Life in the Spirit?

Whatever we may conclude about the nature of the Spirit as recorded in Scripture, if our personal lives are not transformed, our study becomes only an academic matter in which there is no spiritual profit. Contemplation of the blessings conferred through the indwelling of the Spirit is thrilling! While space will not permit an exhaustive treatise of the theme, I want to share with you some of the things we may read in the New Covenant letters.

Ephesians 1:13 , 14 informs us that we are sealed by the Spirit, and the Spirit is God's guarantee that we shall come into our inheritance. These two verses are pregnant with hope for the followers of Jesus. The full text says, "In him you also, who have heard the word of truth, the gospel of your salvation, and have believed in him, were sealed with the promised Holy Spirit, which is the guarantee of our inheritance until we acquire possession of it."

Here we learn that only believers in Christ receive the Spirit as a seal. Only believers will share in the inheritance. This agrees with the words of Jesus, who said the world cannot receive the Spirit because it does not see Him or know Him (John 14:17). In the same verse He declares, concerning His disciples, "You know him, for he dwells with you, and will be in you." Companionship and intimacy are indicated by this expression.

Belief follows the hearing of the word of truth, here defined as the gospel of salvation. In Romans 10:15, 16, the gospel is classified as good news, or glad tidings, and verse 17 says, "So faith comes from what is heard, and what is heard comes by the preaching of Christ." To preach Christ is to proclaim the historical facts related to what He did for men who were lost. Paul declares that the gospel he preached, by which men were saved, was simply that "Christ died for our sins in accordance with the scriptures, that he was buried, that he was raised on the third day in accordance with the scriptures" (1 Corinthians 15:3, 4).

The response of the honest mind to testimony rendered credible is belief of that testimony, faith in what is affirmed. The gospel of Christ is testimony about a Person. It is designed to establish the fact that that Person is the Messiah promised by the prophets. Faith in Christ is belief that He is who He claimed to be. It is more than an acknowledgment of the historicity of the facts, or mental assent to their accuracy. A detached intellectual admission of the factuality is not sufficient. Faith embraces a relationship with the object of belief. Those who receive the Spirit are those who have "believed in him."

The Spirit leads men to salvation by means of a message. It is a message preached by men, heard by men, and believed by men. No theory of salvation by direct operation on the sinner's heart, apart from the Word proclaimed, is given any credence in the Scriptures. There is no historical validation for any person's coming to Christ where missionaries have not taken the message. The Spirit has never created believers except through the announcement of the good news by "earthen vessels." When men react to the testimony by believing in Christ and pledging allegiance to Him, the Spirit moves into the heart where Jesus dwells by faith. There He takes up His abode to act as a seal. The word "seal" is from *sphragis*, a seal or signet that indicated ownership or authenticity. This is important and should not be casually dismissed. Sometimes a seal was in the form of a ring on which was engraved an initial or other identifying mark for stamping documents. We still speak of a "signet ring," which is one bearing the initial of the wearer.

In the days of the apostles, a seal was also used for branding slaves, often on the forehead and in the right hand. Such a brand identified the slave as the possession of the owner. Such a use of the word is found in Revelation 7:2, where an angel appeared from the east with "the seal of the living God." He halted all proceedings until he had sealed the servants of God upon their foreheads and thus marked them as belonging to Him. In Revelation 9:4 mention is made of the suffering endured by those who do not have the seal of God upon their foreheads.

The promised Holy Spirit abiding within the Christian is proof of God's ownership of his person. "But you are not in the flesh, you are in the Spirit, if the Spirit of God really dwells in you. Any one who does not have the Spirit of Christ does not belong to him" (Romans 8:9). The validation of one's claim to be dwelling on the spiritual plane is the indwelling Spirit. The proof that one belongs to Jesus is the seal of the Spirit. One who is conscious that the inner chamber of his being is occupied by this royal Guest need never feel lonely or forsaken. In a remarkable chapter devoted to our relationship to the Spirit, the apostle reaches the height of human thought in three tremendous questions: "What then shall we say to this? If God is for us, who is against us? He who did not spare his own Son but gave him up for us all, will he not also give us all things with him?" (vv. 31, 32).

The Spirit does not simply mark us as being the possession of God, but also acts as a guarantee of our inheritance. With a little thought the reason becomes apparent. The Spirit does not dwell in any except God's children. The Spirit within is proof that the person is a child of God, and an heir of the Father's bounty. In the flesh it is impossible to receive the full measure of the inheritance, but the Spirit is given as a bond of assurance that God will not withhold anything from us.

In our day the word "inheritance" is used for a patrimony received upon the death of a father, but that is not the meaning indicated in the New Covenant Scriptures. Here the word strictly means to receive by lot, and then to receive and possess as one's own. In Matthew 19:29 Jesus speaks of eternal life as an inheritance. This was the life made possible in the eternal kingdom of God, when all that offends or causes sin shall have been eliminated. It is more than unbroken existence. It is also unending joy or bliss.

In Ephesians 5:5 Paul lists certain characters who have no such inheritance in God's kingdom. Those who are walking in the Spirit have such an inheritance awaiting, but they cannot now enjoy it to the fullest because of the limitations of the flesh. The present life is material, subject to decay and mortification. "I tell you this, brethren: flesh and blood cannot inherit the kingdom of God, nor does the perishable inherit the imperishable" (1 Corinthians 15:50).

The indwelling Spirit is the divine guarantee that we shall be changed and brought into the glorious experience of eternal existence. We are not going to be frustrated and defeated. We will not be forsaken. "But our commonwealth is in heaven, and from it we await a Savior, the Lord Jesus Christ, who will change our lowly body to be like his glorious body, by the power which enables him even to subject all things to himself" (Philippians 3:20, 21).

The word rendered "guarantee" in modern versions, and "earnest" in the *King James Version*, is *arrabon*. It was a business term, probably used by Phoenician traders and pawnbrokers who introduced it among the Greeks. It referred to earnest money or other valuable consideration deposited by a prospective purchaser, and forfeited by him if he did not fulfill the agreement. Eventually it came to mean a pledge to carry out a covenant, and in the New Covenant Scriptures it is used only of God's assurance to believers, and never the reverse. In modern Greek "guarantee" is the word for an engagement ring.

From this it will be seen that, although God cannot bestow upon us the full blessing of eternal life while we are in the physical body, He has given us the Holy Spirit as an earnest or pledge that His covenant is certain. I need have no qualm or fear as to my inheritance because the Spirit is God's pledge of my eternal blessedness. As I now share in the Spirit, so will I share in life forever!

The ultimate purpose of human existence is to share in the glory of God. Peter wrote to the persecuted saints that the God of all grace had called them to His eternal glory in Christ. After they had suffered a little while, eternal glory would be theirs (1 Peter 5:10). He told the elders who were faithful in their responsibility they would receive "a crown that fadeth not away" (1 Peter 5:4; KJV). Paul wrote to the Corinthians that the momentary affliction they were enduring was preparing for them "an eternal weight of glory beyond all comparison" (2 Corinthians 4:17). What a comfort to the believer!

To guarantee this culmination of the divine plan for our existence the Spirit abides within us. No one need go down under the burdens of life. Sickness, pain, persecution—God knows about them all, and they will pass away, while for God's children there will be an eternal day. God is in us as the hope of glory.

THE INNER STRENGTH

All of us have known individuals who seem to possess an inner reservoir of strength that never runs dry. Perhaps it is a person against whose frail body all the storms of life have been directed. Poverty, ill health, loss of loved ones—all of these combine to defeat every plan for overcoming the negative forces of life. What is the secret of the overcoming life, the triumphant existence? It cannot be a superior education, for many of these persons have little formal education. It cannot be financial power, for they are often in the throes of penury.

Such people are a constant rebuke to those who talk about luck or fortune making the difference between success or failure. In his book, *On Being a Real Person*, Harry Emerson Fosdick discusses the need for organizing those factors out of which personality can be formed. He points out that we have these factors by nature. After mentioning the various things we need to overcome depression, he deals with the ultimate strength, telling his readers that those whose only method of coping with problems is to rely upon their own strength will eventually face up to a situation where such strength is inadequate and such a method inapplicable.

I know a man who illustrates this very thing. He was once a university instructor, honored and respected by his colleagues, well known for his brilliance. Before he was near retirement age, a series of reverses set in, and these would have ruined a lesser man. His wife was stricken with a lingering disease, and he was forced during a period of many months to watch her die. Left alone, he disposed of his home and moved into an apartment. While he was away on a trip, the building caught fire from faulty wiring, destroying everything he possessed, including his valuable books and manuscripts. These alone represented almost a lifetime of research and writing. Then he became aware of a nervous condition that affected his mobility and disturbed his memory. Finally he had to be placed in a geriatric center where aged patients all about him were awaiting death. Yet, when I went to see him, he was so cheerful and outgoing that he actually helped me. He was alert and interested in what I was doing, and made it appear that all the things that happened to him were really blessings in disguise.

When I could stand it no longer I bluntly asked him what was behind his cheerful attitude. (One of the doctors had told me that this man had transformed the hospital by the radiance of his faith and hope.) He told me the story himself.

He always had been a believer in God, but when he came to the realization that he was alone, sick, and would have to make a complete change of life, he decided to approach the problem with the dynamic of faith. He chose a day to fast and prepare his mind for God's will. He sat down to read the entire book of Psalms to let the courage and hope in these ancient songs of praise seep into his being. He underlined Psalm 121:7, 8: "The Lord will keep you from all evil; he will keep your life. The Lord will keep your going out and your coming in from this time forth and for evermore." He chose this for his motto.

Having walked through the aisles of the book, this once-famous university professor got down on his knees and began to supplicate for God's care. He prayed that God would grant him inward power great enough to overcome every obstacle and enable him to be resigned to the divine will. These are his words: "As I prayed I began to sense a new strength in me that was not my own. I felt a kinship with a force from outside, beyond myself. I retired and slept soundly. I awakened refreshed, confident that the Spirit of God would supply my every need. I believe that during that day of reading and meditation I actually made contact with the power of the Spirit to sustain.''

I became convinced that I was seeing a living demonstration of that for which Paul petitioned in Ephesians 3:14-19. Accordingly, the passage took on a new and fuller meaning for me, and I have been helped immeasurably by thinking about it seriously and often. Here it is for your contemplation, and the best way to share in its wonderful meaning is to savor each clause slowly and carefully:

''For this reason I bow my knees before the Father, from whom every family in heaven and on earth is named, that according to the riches of his glory he may grant you to be strengthened with might through his Spirit in the inner man, and that Christ may dwell in your hearts through faith; that you, being rooted and grounded in love, may have power to comprehend with all the saints what is the breadth and length and height and depth, and to know the love of Christ which surpasses knowledge, that you may be filled with all the fulness of God.''

The human mind is staggered when it seeks to embrace the meaning of this remarkable statement. Who possesses a vocabulary rich enough to describe what it means to be filled with all the fullness of God? Paul has just written that the faithful are built into the holy temple of the Lord, for a dwelling place for the Spirit, and now he assures them that they are recipients of the divine fullness. All that is God's belongs to the saints while they are here, on the conditions enunciated by the apostle.

The first item of the petition is that believers may be strengthened with might by the Spirit in the inner man. No one who accepts the Scripture as a divine revelation can doubt that the human being consists of both an outer and inner man. In Romans 7:22, 23, Paul identifies the inmost self with the mind or heart. It is possible for one of God's children to grow stronger in the faith even as he grows weaker in the body. The Spirit does not abide in us to keep the flesh always youthful. The passing of years takes a toll of the flesh. The promise is that though our outer nature wears away our inner nature is being renewed every day (2 Corinthians 4:16).

The versatile Greek language was especially endowed with words for "power." Two of these are found in the terms "strengthened" and "might." The first is from *kratos*, power that is manifested or applied. The root from which it is derived means to perfect or complete, and was connected with creative ability or energy.

"Might" is from *dunamis*, familiar to us in such English words as dynamic, dynamo, and dynamite. When used in contrast with other synonyms, it generally referred to inherent power. In this instance it signifies the power that is natural to the Spirit of God.

With these facts before us, it is apparent that the apostle was asking God to manifest the divine dynamic, the spirit of creative energy and power in the lives of the saints, and to do so on the basis of the riches of His glory. This means nothing less than the fact that believers in Christ Jesus, filled with the Spirit, are furnished the power to do all that God expects of them in the universe. Instead of being weak, vacillating creatures, battered by the winds of fate, they are more victorious than conquerors, through Him who loved us.

Sometimes we speak in awe of the Christian heroes who have arisen in times of crisis to leave their marks upon the world and the church. Almost invariably, these were common men, reared in humble circumstances. They met the needs of the hour when they realized that God dwelt in them through His Spirit, providing them the power to offset the evil forces that confronted them. The same Spirit abides in us all. We are not all called to become reformers like Luther and Zwingli, but we are called to serve in our localities and according to our capacities. For this, God provides an inner dynamic that cannot know defeat.

The tragedy of our generation is wasted lives because of late awakening. We discover the royal provision too late to employ it effectively. The creative energy that framed this majestic universe dwells in us and is ours to use. A remarkable statement is found in Ephesians 1:19, 20, in which Paul asserts that the same power God used to raise Jesus from the dead is ours now: "And what is the immeasurable greatness of his power in us who believe, according to the working of his great might which he accomplished in Christ when he raised him from the dead and made him sit at his right hand in the heavenly places."

What a startling difference it would make in our Christian witness today, if we actually believed in the dynamic strength of the indwelling Spirit. Sermons would catch on fire. Churches would march with zeal. Homes would be transformed. How sad it is to see men and women living in spiritual poverty when the Father has deposited a great treasure to our account out of the riches of His glory. We need not beg for this power. It is ours now! We do not have to plead with God to do what He has already done. Having power available in a house will not provide light until we plug in to the power. That is all we need to do now through faith and absolute trust in God.

The apostle prayed "that Christ may dwell in your hearts by faith." The word "dwell" is used of abiding relationships. Another word is employed for one who drops in for a casual visit. "Dwell" is used to signify one who moves in as a permanent part of the household. Jesus seeks to become one with us, to establish himself as the guiding factor in life. Faith is the reaching out of the human heart to seal the relationship by which Heaven becomes real to us.

Paul also would have those who are in Christ possess the ability to grasp the potential of that love which is the most powerful force in the universe. In order to do this they must be rooted and grounded in love. Although both of these have to do with foundational matters, they regard the life of the disciple of Christ from different perspectives.

"Rooted" makes us think of our lives as growing and developing plants. This is a common metaphor throughout the Bible! Men are often spoken of as trees planted by the divine hand. Often the trees used in such symbolism are fruit trees, and the kind of soil in which they are planted will help to determine the quality of fruit produced. It is essential that we put down the roots of faith into that love which can stand against all erosive forces. "Love bears all things and endures all things."

"Grounded" makes us consider human life as a building or structure. This picture also occurs frequently in Scripture. A building is as secure as its foundation, and no foundation is more solid than enduring love. The love here mentioned is not an emotion or sentiment, but an act of will. It is never accidental or incidental. It is purposeful and voluntary. And it is always active, never passive.

We must start out with faith and love, and we must never outgrow or abandon either. Everything that is said must be spoken in faith and love. Everything that is done must be performed in faith and love. We must begin by going down into the soil of love. We must continue by growing up in love. The Spirit dwelling within us is a royal guest in a temple making all of this possible. Indeed, the Spirit is the very source of that love, providing a hope that will never end in disappointment or disillusionment. "And hope does not disappoint us, because God's love has been poured into our hearts through the Holy Spirit which has been given to us" (Romans 5:5).

God's love is not our love for God; it is rather the love that God is (1 John 4:16). The testimony is plain: "Love is of God, and he who loves is born of God and knows God. He who does not love does not know God; for God is love" (4:7, 8). If we would be like God, if we would give evidence that we have been born of God and know God, we must manifest the love of God. We cannot develop or generate this love while we are caught up in the human predicament.

The fleshly nature—selfish, egotistical, and egocentric—rebels against genuine concern for the involvement in the needs of others. It always asks, "What is in it for me?" Its philosophy is, "Let him get his like I got mine." The fleshly nature (or selfishness) is the attitude of the priest and Levite, not that of the good Samaritan.

To turn over a new leaf is not enough. We must turn up with a new life. This means that there must be a change from the human nature to the divine, and this is the work of the Spirit. "His divine power has granted to us all things that pertain to life and godliness, through the knowledge of him who called us to his own glory and excellence, by which he has granted to us his precious and very great promises, that through these you may escape from the corruption that is in the world because of passion, and become partakers of the divine nature" (2 Peter 1:3, 4).

If you open your heart and life to the ministrations of the Spirit of God, your changed life will be one of the greatest blessings that you have ever known. You will become more like Jesus, and the divine love flowing through your personality will touch and change and cleanse those around you. Members of your own family, the people with whom you work, your friends and neighbors—all will recognize that you are living on a different plane, and that life has taken on a new perspective. God made you and He wants you to be a vessel fit for the use for which He designed you.

If you are a physician you must become God's practitioner. If you are a truck driver you must become God's truck driver. The Bible knows nothing about "professional ministers." It recognizes the work of "ministering professionals." College teachers, farmers, dentists, taxi drivers, nurses, and housewives must all have the same vocation or calling: the calling of God. What they do to make a living is not their vocation, but their avocation. God calls you to serve where you are, but He does not call you to flounder around helplessly. He furnishes the power by which you can fulfill your purpose.

You do not need to quit what you are doing to "enter the ministry." You entered the ministry when you came into Christ. The power to perform that ministry was yours from the moment Christ, through the Spirit, entered you. Recognition of this will produce a sense of happiness and well-being you never knew before. Open your life to God's will and purpose. Tune your personality to vibrate in unison with the divine. You will find that life will take on a completely new dimension, and your feet will be planted on higher ground.

Perhaps nothing is more detrimental to the cause of Christ than the idea that some of God's people should be urged to enter "full-time service." The very term suggests that the great majority are only part-time servants. This has led to the concept that those who volunteer "full time" must have a greater degree of dedication and commitment than others. Even their behavior and style of life must be different. They must deny themselves certain things counted as luxuries, while others can pile them up. They are expected to live dynamic and energetic lives for Jesus while those who support them can exist in a powerless spiritual condition.

This is foreign to the Scriptures. It is not only unscriptural but antiscriptural. The idea of asking Christians to volunteer for full-time work for Jesus after they have been in Him for ten years is absurd. No one can enlist for part-time work in the kingdom of God. No provision is made for goldbricks or fill-in laborers. In Christ, life is service, and service is life. One who does not enlist full time is preparing to be dead the greater part of the time!

The Spirit dwells in every child of God and dwells in all of them for the same purpose, though not for the same function. The function of each is determined by his ability, talent, or gift, coupled with opportunity. The purpose of the Spirit is to furnish each one the dynamic to accomplish the work for which he is adapted. There are no useless members. God has added each to the body as He pleases.

A mistaken view exists about making a witness for Jesus. Some persons feel they must quit their employment in order to obey God's Word for their lives. If one is working in an endeavor that is sinful in itself, or in which his conscience condemns him, he should get out of it. But one who makes his living in a legitimate business is working for God. The same Word that urges faithfulness to God also says, "Study to be quiet, and to do your own business, and to work with your own hands, as we commanded you; that ye may walk honestly toward them that are without, and that ye may have lack of nothing" (1 Thessalonians 4:11, 12; KJV).

This is the instruction of the Spirit, and surely He will empower those who heed it. Some may feel called to leave an occupation and preach the Word of

God to those who have not heard it. This is good. Others who may not have the ability to do that may remain in the shop or office. One is no more a minister of God than the other. They simply serve in different places, but all must serve in the Spirit.

FRUIT OF THE SPIRIT

Closely akin to this is the teaching of God's revelation on the fruit of the Spirit. The word for fruit is *karpos*, defined as that which is produced by the inherent energy of a living organism. In a spiritual sense, W. E. Vine says that it is "the visible expression of power working inwardly and invisibly, the character of the fruit being evidence of the character of the power producing it."

In His dissertation on the Spirit as a helper, Jesus inserted the metaphor of the vine and the branches (John 15:1-10). In this appropriate illustration God is the gardener, and Jesus the true vine. The branches are His followers. "Herein is my Father glorified, that ye bear much fruit; so shall ye be my disciples" (John 15:8; KJV). Some things are made clear in the metaphor. One is that the branch is helpless to bear fruit of itself. Jesus said, "The branch cannot bear fruit of itself, except it abide in the vine" (v. 4; KJV).

A branch does not produce grapes, but becomes the channel through which fruit is borne. It is the inward strength derived through union with the vine that makes fruit possible. As Jesus put it, "Without me ye can do nothing." The will of God for a human life can never be carried out separated from Jesus

147

Christ. Men deceive themselves when they think they can achieve righteousness on their own. Just as the sap enlivens the vine and produces fruit, so the Spirit results in the fruit that pleases God in a human life.

As recorded in Philippians 1:9, Paul prayed that the love of the brethren would grow ever richer and richer in knowledge and insight of every kind, bringing upon them the gift of true discrimination. By this means they would be able to produce the full fruit of righteousness through Jesus Christ.

One need not be barren and unfruitful. A life of uselessness is a reflection upon God who created us to produce fruit and will make it possible for us to do so if we remain in Him. Jesus once condemned a fig tree, for it had "nothing but leaves." Our excuses are generally attempts to escape from reality and responsibility. We seek to make it appear that everything depends upon ourselves, when it is God who works in us to will and to do His good pleasure if we allow Him to do so.

A farmer taking care of a rock-strewn, hilly acreage in the Missouri Ozarks was reading his Bible one day while his team rested in the shade. For the first time in his life the message got through to him that every Christian had a responsibility to call others to the side of Christ, and that God would work in and with one who boldly testified of his faith. At noon that day he told his wife they must sell out and move. She was startled by this hasty decision. He explained that he had but little formal education and could not do a great deal among local people who knew more than himself. He reasoned that somewhere there were those more ignorant than he, and he could teach them and earn their gratitude.

Each day he prayed for God to show him where he should go. Two years later he found himself in the far north in an Eskimo fishing village. He purchased a boat, staffed it with natives, and on their first trip led them all to faith in Jesus. In a few brief years the people in two villages had become believers and had been trained to carry on for Christ and tell others the story. The one-time farmer now felt the urge to go to "regions beyond."

He entered the African bush country where missionaries had seldom appeared. He and his wife denied themselves the finer things of life to share with others. Although he could never speak the native tongues, he found willing, if sometimes inept, translators who could get the gist of the message through while the teacher drew diagrams in the dust with a stick. He often went into remote villages and leaned against the wheel of an ox wagon and talked through the entire day as his students squatted about him. His wife ministered to the sick and distressed. As a result, they adopted and reared two native babies whose mothers died in childbirth.

I met the aged couple in London while they were en route to the United States on their first visit back home in more than twenty years. I spent several days with them, and my own faith was deepened by this encounter. These saints of God were quite uneducated and would have been turned down by any examining committee or screening board for missionaries. Yet they had reached thousands of persons for Christ and converted whole villages. The work was being carried on in their absence by the two black children they had reared. These children were so thoroughly trained in the Scriptures that, even though hardly sixteen years of age, they could supervise the effort for Christ.

The aged and wrinkled missionary told me that it seemed almost by chance that, on the day his life was transformed into a worker for Christ on that Missouri farm, he connected in his mind two passages from God's Word: "Without me ye can do nothing . . . I can do all things through Christ which strengtheneth me" (John 15:5; Philippians 4:13; KJV). He never forgot these, and they remained his motto all of his life. He has long since gone to be with the Lord, but his fruit is still being gathered. "I knew that somewhere there were people more ignorant than myself, and if I could find them I could teach them." He found them on two continents and brought forth fruit among them. In spite of my own firm confidence in the Word of God, I always find myself greatly humbled by those who achieve so much regardless of educational handicaps, through simple, trusting faith.

The real productivity of the Spirit is best evidenced in a remarkable statement to the Galatians, in which the apostle contrasts the works of the flesh and the fruit of the Spirit. You will find the record in Galatians 5:1-16. Although several items are listed under each category, the term "works" is plural, while the singular form is used for the fruit of the Spirit. Life in the Spirit does not consist of the exhibition of certain virtues, but of a unified and harmonious existence under God's marvelous grace.

Verse 16 urges the Galatians to "walk in the Spirit, and ye shall not fulfil the lust of the flesh." It is essential that "the flesh" here be properly identified, because there is a tendency to think of it only in connection with sexual sins. This is encouraged by the use of the word "lust" in the Authorized Version. Such a limitation is not justifiable in this chapter. Many of the "works of the flesh" have no connection with sensuality or sex. One may walk in the flesh by engaging in "envy, fits of rage, selfish ambitions, and party intrigues," as certainly as if he indulged in fornication and indecency.

"The flesh" is simply "the lower nature," and the word is so translated in the New English Version. The flesh is man pursuing his own stubborn way, rejecting the guidance of the Spirit, and resisting the lordship of Jesus. It is life undisciplined and unrestrained by the power of God, asserting itself without reference to the divine will or purpose. Men who never committed an act of sexual impropriety may be walking in the flesh as certainly as the most flagrant adulterer.

It is not necessary to list all the things that enslave men and make them victims of the material and perishable. Paul does not consider the catalogue complete, seeing that he closes with the words, "and such like." Of one thing he is certain: Those who do such things will never inherit the kingdom of God. The Spirit is the key to the inheritance, and "they that are Christ's have crucified the [lower nature] with the affections and lusts" (Galatians 5:24; KJV).

The fruit of the Spirit is love, joy, peace, patience, kindness, goodness, faith, gentleness, and self-control. The heart pulsates with spiritual vitality in its contemplation of these noble attributes. They are the result of a transformed personality, and they could transform the world. No law exists to rebuke these. They can never be had in excess. There can never be too much love, joy, patience, or kindness. One need not limit goodness or faith. The more gentleness and self-control one has the better he will be, and the greater blessing he will be to those about him. The Spirit will produce this fruit in all who are committed to His power and strength. God be praised!

9

Slavery or Freedom?

A book, like human life on earth, must come to an end. This is true whether the book (or the life) is good or bad. If the content of this final chapter achieves its purpose, it will make your life better. The message will substitute faith for frustration and hope for hopelessness. It will take you by the hand and lead you in the path God has marked out through the "garden of prayer." And it will give meaning and power to your existence on earth.

This chapter will be devoted to a discussion of things mentioned in one chapter of the New Covenant Scriptures. Romans 8 can be called the chapter of the Holy Spirit. Every chapter in the Bible is such by origin, but this chapter deserves the designation because of content. It is a marvelous presentation of the blessings to be derived from the indwelling Spirit, an oasis for the earth-dweller who must wander through the desert with a desperate need for refreshment. If Martin Luther was correct in regarding Romans as the Alps of the Bible, this chapter is the highest peak, sublime in its towering majesty.

Recently I talked with a young man, a graduate from college, who had returned after a period of service abroad in the armed forces. He had started out to be a Christian while a mere lad, but when he was thrown into rough company away from home he allowed the temptations of the flesh to overcome him.

He was unhappy, filled with remorse because he was living contrary to every principle he had been taught by godly parents. He felt powerless in the grip of sin and loneliness. One night, alone in his quarters, he opened the Bible for want of something to do, and by chance he began reading Romans 8. So powerfully was he impressed that he got up, went outside and walked under the stars, promising God that he would allow the Spirit to take over and command his life from that time on. Reinforced by this indwelling Helper, he returned home stronger than he was when he went away.

There is something tremendous about a chapter that can cleanse and purify lives in this manner. I know that, while I do not comprehend everything involved in this glorious chapter written by Paul, I have grasped enough of it to realize that it holds the divine secret for a power-packed life. I never read it without being elevated in heart. Romans 8 is God's chairlift to take me from the valley to the peak where I can breathe the pure air of Heaven and look down upon the smog.

Here the Spirit of the Lord becomes my friend and companion. Surely one who lives in the same apartment with another should come to know him. The Holy Spirit has moved in to the inner room of my tenement. He has taken down the "empty" sign and become the occupant together with my spirit. Now I am never lonely, for I am never alone. I do not feel forsaken or forlorn! I am happy in the knowledge that the heavenly visitor shares my abode. Let us look at what it really means to entertain this royal guest.

FREEDOM FROM CONDEMNATION

Perhaps no other thought brings a greater sense of despair to man than that of the condemnation hanging over him because of his sin. Life itself becomes a prison cell in which he is a captive awaiting death, and that is the foretaste of everlasting doom. But to be freed from dread, to know that death is conquered—that is a blessing almost indescribable. Yet, the apostle assures us "There is therefore now no condemnation to them which are in Christ Jesus, who walk not after the flesh, but after the Spirit" (Romans 8:1; KJV). Out of Christ, condemnation reigns and man is under the sentence of death. In Christ there is no condemnation. Out of Christ men walk according to the flesh. In Christ they walk according to the Spirit.

To "walk after the flesh" means more than simply to cater to passion. It entails this, but it means to live in such a state that Christ is left out of consideration. He is ignored. Decisions are made, and steps are taken without recourse to the demands of God. No authority is recognized except that of one's own wish and pleasure. On the other hand, to walk after the Spirit is to be ever conscious of the will and direction of God, regardless of the cost.

"For to be carnally minded is death; but to be spiritually minded is life and peace" (Romans 8:6; KJV); I think I may have talked about that for years before I really understood the profound truth embodied in it. The carnal mind simply discards God. Denial of the existence of God is not necessary. All that is necessary is to act as though God is not there,

155

and to order one's existence with no thought of the divine will. The carnal mind thinks only in terms of the present. It asks immediate gratification and discounts the idea of any future reckoning. Because it looks forward to nothing, it grasps greedily at the now. It dies today for it has no tomorrow.

The Spirit changes all of that. He provides a happy yesterday because of memory without regret, a glorious today in the experience of God's joyful love, and a wonderful anticipation of tomorrow in a state of blessedness. Peace can be disturbed by the thought of past sins, present suffering, or future punishment. The spiritual mind, being free from all of these, has life and peace.

DEATH OF UNRIGHTEOUSNESS

Anyone who has wrestled with some evil tendency knows the agony of his trying to overcome it while the flesh cries out for gratification. Paul described the condition by saying, "To will is present with me; but how to perform that which is good I find not" (7:18; KJV). God made us, loves us, and knows more about our nature than we do. For that reason He has not left us to grapple alone with the problem.

In the first place, Jesus paid the full obligation we owe to the flesh. The debt of sin was canceled by His blood. "Therefore, brethren, we are debtors, not to the flesh, to live after the flesh" (8:12). I do not owe sinful human nature one thing. I am free from every debt it once held against me. No sin can have any rightful claim upon my life. I have been bought with a price and so I no longer belong to myself.

In the second place, God has invested me with His Spirit to put to death the evil deeds that once enticed me. Listen! "For if ye live after the flesh, ye shall die: but if ye through the Spirit do mortify the deeds of the body, ye shall live" (v. 13). We sometimes use the word mortify in these days to indicate embarrassment. We may use such an expression as, "I was mortified by the language he used in my presence." But that is not the meaning of the word in the Scriptures.

Mortus means death. A mortal wound results in death. A mortician prepares the bodies of the dead. A mortuary is a place where the corpses may be viewed. To mortify means to kill. Paul is simply saying that the power of the indwelling Spirit of God enables us to put to death the evil passions and corrupt desires.

In recent years those who had been addicted to drugs have occasionally testifed that when they surrendered wholly and completely to Christ and turned their lives over to God, they were able immediately to conquer the dread habit without any physical withdrawal symptoms. This was seriously questioned by men in the medical profession, and research projects were inaugurated in some cases to determine the accuracy of the reports. In several cases it was found that former addicts were telling the truth about their victory. One research team reported, "Our investigation indicated that those who testified to immediate conquest of the addiction when subjected to a religious experience of deep significance were stating a fact. It was as if some powerful inner force was operative, enabling them to overcome the need to which they had been subjected and of which they been victims."

The Holy Spirit is that "powerful inner force" and dwells in men to help them glorify God in both body and spirit. A man who had grown up in a home where profanity was a way of communication, found himself powerless to overcome the habit, for it had become natural to him. When he turned himself over to Jesus, he prayed for divine help. He said that he felt as though his heart had been scrubbed clean and his tongue had been purged. His manner of speech was transformed. The Spirit had put to death the deeds of the body.

Another man had become a compulsive gambler, and had wrecked his home, forcing away his wife and little son. He was led to believe in Jesus by a former gambling companion who had found an answer for his own life in the Son of God. The man who had neglected his home, his business, and all else to sit at the gambling table, now implored not only divine mercy but divine aid. He was serious about it and from the time he gave himself to Christ Jesus he no longer felt the need to engage in games of chance. On the contrary, he became a living example of the rescued life. He was thrilled when I told him that Christians were known in the world of the early Greeks as "the gamblers" because they were willing to risk everything, including life on earth, to follow Jesus as the Lord of life.

It does not seem advisable to leave this line of thought without pointing out the statement immediately following the expression, "If ye through the Spirit do mortify the deeds of the body, ye shall live." The very next sentence is "For as many as are led by the Spirit of God, they are the sons of God." The word "for" joins the two sentences and demonstrates that we are able to overcome the baser passions and desires. We have a relationship to the Father in which the Spirit becomes the energizing power enabling us to become more like God.

Think of the implications in the phrase "led by the Spirit of God." The original for "led" is *ago*. Two things can be said of its usage in the New Covenant Scriptures. First, it generally applies to persons, and has to do with their motivation to act. Second, it implies willingness and cooperation on the part of those who are led. The leading is not by force. It is not against the will. To be led by the Spirit is to surrender to the influence and guidance of the Spirit. This is a proof of divine sonship. Only sons of God will be led by the Spirit, and thus, when one is so led he has a personal relationship with God. This is quite different from the measuring rods employed by men.

Jesus placed the term "son of God" on a higher plane, morally, than a mere tie of relationship with the Father. There are certain characteristics stated as conditions. For example, only peacemakers can be truly regarded as children of God. This is brought out by Jesus in Matthew 5:9. If one belongs to a religious organization and has a good knowledge of Scripture, yet is guilty of sowing discord among brethren or of refusing to labor for peace, he cannot be called a child of God. True children of God wage peace as actively as others wage war.

Again, Jesus postulates love, even for those who despitefully use you and are enemies, as the criterion of sonship. He says, "Love your enemies, . . . and pray for them which . . . persecute you; that ye may be the children of your Father which is in heaven" (Matthew 5:44; KJV). Love for those who are hostile toward God and ourselves is not simply the best policy, or the way of kindness and pacifism. Love is an essential of the divine-human relationship. This kind of love is a fruit of the Spirit. Not simply an outgrowth of temperament, it is shed abroad in our hearts by the Holy Spirit. The sons of God are those who are led, directed, motivated by, and filled with the Spirit of God. What a triumph over the flesh when one can walk in the Spirit, that is, when every step he takes is in the atmosphere created by the Spirit. Thus, we glorify God.

WITNESS TO SONSHIP

Romans 8:15-17 is one of the most comforting passages in the revelation of God. It is so filled with beauty and majesty that perhaps most persons who read it will go through life without ever probing its depths. Read it and meditate upon it:

"For ye have not received the spirit of bondage again to fear; but ye have received the Spirit of adoption, whereby we cry, Abba, Father. The Spirit itself beareth witness with our spirit, that we are the children of God: and if children, then heirs; heirs of God, and joint-heirs with Christ; if so be that we suffer with him, that we may be also glorified together"(KJV).

The spiritual implications of a term are difficult to understand if one is not familiar with its natural relationships. In our culture, "the spirit of bondage" may be passed over lightly by a modern reader. We have never experienced the agony of physical slavery and cannot fully appreciate "the spirit of slavery" as applied to sin. On the contrary, we may regard the life of sin as a pleasant time of indulgence that we are called upon to give up or "sacrifice" for Jesus Christ. Thus, the life in Christ is actually regarded as a bondage to which we surrender ourselves, more or less reluctantly, in order to secure a reward.

This was not the case with the citizens of Rome. One writer tells us that the period which witnessed the early growth of Christianity was one of horror and degradation unequalled in the history of mankind. Of the state of things in Rome at this time, Canon Farrar writes, "At the lowest extreme of the social scale were millions of slaves without family, without religion, without possessions, who had no recognized rights, and towards whom none had any recognized duties, passing normally from a childhood of degradation to a manhood of hardship, and an old age of unpitied neglect."[11]

The French historian Du Pape declares that it can be fairly well authenticated that there were sixty million slaves in the Roman Empire when the gospel was first proclaimed. We are indebted to Cornelius Tacitus, the Roman historian, born the year Paul began his third preaching tour, for the information that the slaves were so numerous they were divided and registered according to their nationalities. And

Seneca, the philosopher, the brother of Gallio before whom Paul was brought (Acts 18:12), writes that every slave was under a constant cloud of suspicion as a potential enemy.

To illustrate the enduring fear associated with slavery, I need mention only one incident recorded by Tacitus. The Roman Senate was debating the murder of Pedanius Secundus by one of his slaves. C. Cassius Longinus arose and gravely argued for enforcement of the Silanian law, which made it mandatory to kill all of the slaves owned by a master who was murdered. One after another of the senators came to the rostrum to vote for this sanguinary law. Remembering that such masters often owned hundreds of slaves and that these were in constant jeopardy by the act of one hothead or brutal criminal, one can see how cheaply life was regarded by the patricians or ruling classes.

The citizens of Rome could make an immediate application of Paul's statement to the fear of slavery and degradation of sin. The fact is that his letter was written just the year before the meeting of the Senate described by Tacitus. Nothing was glamorous about slavery. Slaves were sustained only by the faint hope of freedom, or by the certain hope of death.

While we are a long way from the conditions so described, we can still offer a few suggestions about "the spirit of slavery" to sin from which we have been set free by the grace of God.

(1) Slavery to sin destroys human dignity, reducing one to the animal level, making him a victim of passion and inordinate desire. Peter writes, "But these, as natural brute beasts, made to be taken and

destroyed, speak evil of the things that they understand not; and shall utterly perish in their own corruption" (2 Peter 2:12; KJV).

(2) Slavery to sin demands all of our powers and resources, and places every faculty under tribute. Sin reigning in our mortal bodies exacts obedience to the body's desires. It forces us to put all of our parts at its disposal as instruments for wrongdoing (Romans 6:12, 13). Sin is the most cruel taskmaster in the universe.

(3) Slavery to sin reduces us to servitude and then pays off with death. Sin promises everything and provides nothing. "When ye were the servants of sin, ye were free from righteousness. What fruit had ye then in those things whereof ye are now ashamed? for the end of those things is death" (vv. 20, 21; KJV).

(4) Slavery to sin brings only misery and despair. "We know that the law is spiritual: but I am carnal, sold under sin . . . O wretched man that I am! who shall deliver me from the body of this death?" (7:14, 24).

(5) Slavery to sin forces its captives to breathe the polluted and poisonous atmosphere of fear. All of their lifetime they are subject to bondage through fear of death (Hebrews 2:15), and fear brings the dread of approaching judgment (1 John 4:18).

Over against the frightful state conjured up in the mind at mention of this "spirit of slavery" is another term, "the spirit of adoption." No more significant expression could be used to indicate a complete transformation in the Roman mind. From slavery to adoption would be like a Horatio Alger book,

From Rags to Riches. Only if we understand the legal adoptive process can we ever grasp what the apostle is saying. Fortunately, there has been preserved in Roman laws a mass of material related to the adoption process, a very serious business in Rome.

Notice the use of the expression, "very serious business" with reference to Roman adoptive procedures. It was made especially serious because of the law called *patria potestas*. This law gave a father absolute authority over his offspring as long as they lived. It conferred upon the father the right to punish a son regardless of the son's age. He could kill his son and no one could lift a finger against him.

In 450 B.C. a revolt developed among the common people against the patricians. They alleged that the patricians abused the unwritten law and took advantage of them, denying them their civil rights. The magistrates, in order to avoid a revolution, were commissioned to draw up a code, inscribing it upon ten tablets. These were accepted by the popular assembly. Later two more tablets were added to make the great body of laws known as *Lex Duodecim Tabularium,* the "law of the twelve tablets." The laws became the supreme law of the land.

The *patria potestas* stemmed from the second stipulation of the fourth tablet. It provided for the control of a father over his children. His right existed during their whole life to imprison, scourge, keep to rustic labor in chains, to sell or slay, even though they may have been high state officials. A son could not own land in his own name as long as his father lived.

We must try to catch the atmosphere in Rome

when Paul wrote to the Romans about slavery and adoptions. In order to do this I shall insert a quotation from Dionysius of Halicarnassus. His testimony is especially valuable because he was a Greek historian living in Rome at the time Augustus issued his decree for the whole Roman Empire to enroll for taxation puposes. Dionysius wrote *Roman Antiquities*, a twenty-volume history of his adopted city. Nine of these have been preserved in their entirety, and in one of them is this description of the *patria potestas*:

> "The law-giver of the Romans gave virtually full power to the father over his son, whether he thought proper to imprison him, to scourge him, to put him in chains, and keep him at work in the fields, or to put him to death; and this even though the son was already engaged in public affairs, though he were numbered among the highest magistrates, and though he were celebrated for his zeal for the commonwealth. Indeed in virtue of this law men of distinction while delivering speeches from the rostra, hostile to the senate and pleasing to the people, and enjoying great popularity on that account, have been dragged down from thence, and carried away by their fathers, to undergo such punishment as these thought fit; and while they were being led away through the forum, none present, neither counsul, tribune, nor the very populace which was flattering them, and thought all power inferior to its own, could rescue them."[11]

Adoption involved the transfer of a person from the absolute control of his whole life by one man to

---

[11]Frederic W. Farrar, D.D., F.R.S., *The Early Days of Christianity* (London: Cassell and Co., 1884), p. 2.

the absolute control of his life by another. There had to be a complete surrender of the power of life and death by one and a complete assumption of that power by another. So drastic was this change that the one who was transferred to another *patria potestas* was looked upon as a wholly new creature. He was said to be born again, or born anew. A whole new existence began for him on the day the transfer of allegiance was ratified. Never again would he be subject in any sense to his former relationship. It was as if he had literally died to his past.

The ceremony of adoption was always public, requiring at least five witnesses. There were two parts to it. The first was called *mancipatio*. From this we get our word emancipate, which means to transfer ownership. It derives from *manus*, hand; and *capero*, to take. In a sale, an article was taken in hand by the new owner. In *mancipatio* the father, the child, and the prospective father took their places with five witnesses upon the dais in the Forum. One of these, called the *librapens* (bearer of the scales) held a pair of balances in one hand and a short brass rod in the other.

The prospective father said, "This day I purchase your son for my own." He then placed a coin in one pan of the balance. The father placed the son's hand in the other pan, but before the sale could be completed he removed the boy's hand, and the other removed his coin. This identical procedure was again enacted. But the third time the father did not remove the hand of the son. The scales were struck with the brass rod as a sign that the sale was completed. The coin was given to the boy as a sign that he would inherit from the new father. It was a seal of his relationship. Even to this day, we say, "The third time is the charm."

There remained one more step called *vindicatio*. In Roman law this meant to affirm and assert one's legal right to a thing. The new father took the adopted son to a magistrate and had his new name properly inscribed in the census tables and the right of *patria potestas*, of life and death, passed into his hands. All of this is most interesting to me, but it is secondary to the purpose of the apostle Paul. His primary desire is to impress upon the Romans the great blessings that accrue to us in Christ. The privileges that were bestowed by adoption in Rome included:

(1) The one adopted was ushered into a whole new family relationship, with a new father and new brothers and sisters, and this was the direct result of the father's choice. He was a chosen one, an elected person. The word "adoption" means to choose, as our word *option* indicates.

(2) The one adopted was given a new name, clearly indicative of his new relationship.

(3) The adopted one was permitted to eat at the father's table, a privilege never accorded slaves. In the Greek world such eating together was an expression of *koinonia*, fellowship, the sharing of the common life of the father and his family.

(4) He became heir of the estate of the father. If there was an elder brother he became a joint heir with him. He shared in both the hardships and rewards of the family, for this was part of their common life, the fellowship.

(5) When one was adopted by Roman law, his past life was literally blotted out. His former name was removed from the roster of citizenship. All debts were canceled, all obligations deleted. The adopted person began a new life with the slate wiped clean. Even his education began anew. Cicero said the aim of this education was to produce "self-control, combined with dutiful affection to parents and kindliness to kindred."

Paul speaks of the Spirit in connection with the cry "Abba, Father." He says that we did not receive the spirit of slavery to promote fear, but the Spirit of adoption to enable us to utter these lovely words. Two passages contain the expression "Abba, Father." According to Romans 8:15 the Spirit enables us to say these words. Galatians 4:6 records that the Spirit thus cries out. In both cases our divine sonship is under consideration. We are adopted, that is, given the place of a son. Adoption is from *huiothesis*, to place as a son. Because we are inducted into the glorious family we are able to cry, "Abba, Father." That is, we are able, through the Spirit, to recognize our real relationship to Christ.

There is more to it than this. The word *abba* could not have been translated "father." It is an Aramaic word, and was the first expression of a little child in the East. In our country little children say "Da-da" or "Pa-pa" and we must transliterate with "Daddy" and "Papa" to indicate that these are the simple, unaffected, and spontaneous expressions of love in early life. We could not capture this meaning to translate by supplying the word "father."

Paul knew well that the Jews had a strict law

forbidding a slave to use the word "abba" in addressing a master or the head of a household. So when he wants to show that we are sons, and not slaves, he makes it clear that the indwelling Spirit identifies us as children of God and makes it possible for us to speak to the Father in a fashion that slaves were not allowed to use. And so close is the union between the Holy Spirit and my own spirit that only the Father can discern which one is calling out to Him.

But the Spirit not only makes it possible for me to cry Abba, but also Father. The first is the cry of emotion and feeling, the tender call of a little child. The second is the form of address of a mature person. W. E. Vine points out that the last word is a wholly different form of address, and that it indicates an intelligent recognition of the relationship sustained with the one so addressed. The word "father" involves confidence and obedience, and when taken with the other word shows a relationship of love and intelligent trust.

But we are told that "the Spirit itself beareth witness with our spirit, that we are the children of God: and if children, then heirs; heirs of God, and joint-heirs with Christ" (Romans 8:16, 17; KJV). What does this tremendous statement mean? Remember that Paul is contrasting the state of slavery with the superb experience of sonship. I have described for you the public ceremony of adoption. The sale of a slave, having many of the same aspects, also took place in the presence of witnesses and involved a pair of balances and a deposit of money in one of the pans of the balance.

Suppose the father of an adopted child died, and

the natural sons hated the one who was adopted and wanted to debar him from his inheritance. They could claim that he was never adopted at all, but was simply purchased as a slave. The adopted son would have to bring a witness to corroborate his own testimony. If he could find the *librapens*, the scales bearer, that one could say, "I was present, and I know he is a son because I struck the brass ingot and sealed the transaction."

The Holy Spirit exists in us for that very purpose. He is a seal of my redemption. "Now he which stablisheth us with you in Christ, and hath anointed us, is God; who hath also sealed us, and given the earnest of the Spirit in our hearts" (2 Corinthians 1:21, 22; KJV).

The indwelling Spirit is God's guarantee that I am going to inherit every provision of grace. I am not a slave. I am a son. My spirit testifies of this. The Holy Spirit testifies the same. I am even a joint heir with Christ. This establishes the quality of our sonship. Whatever is the lot of Jesus is to be my lot. We are "sharers together" with everything that sonship involves. This is the matter to which the Spirit witnesses.

When Paul affirms that the Spirit bears witness with our spirit that we are children of God, he assures us that the testimony of our spirit and the Holy Spirit is that we are not sold into slavery. We have been adopted in the majestic family of our Father in Heaven. The promise of Jesus that He would not leave us orphans has come true. Two witnesses within proclaim this fact: the spirit of man and the Spirit of God.

HELP IN WEAKNESS

The difference between one's being in Christ Jesus and being on the outside is hope. It is not that those on the outside do not have hope, for all men do. The difference lies in the varying degree of intensity. Those who know the Lord find their hope increasing as they grow older. Those who do not know Him find their hope waning, and frequently being supplanted by two malign evils to personality—dread and despair.

Every rational person realizes that he is not going to get out of the human predicament alive. All of his plans for postponing the inevitable are doomed. His string is going to run out. The thread is going to be snipped. The Christian "sustained by an unfaltering trust" is able to "wrap the drapery of his couch about him and lie down to pleasant dreams." Not so the one who sins away his day of grace and suddenly faces the blackness of hopelessness. Without hope we are of all men most miserable.

What is hope? The simplest definition is "a joyous anticipation of the future." Although hope is related to expectation they are not the same. One may expect bad as well as good, storm as well as sunshine. Only when expectation is accompanied by desire is the ingredient of hope included. We desire some things we do not expect, and expect some things we do not desire, but when we have desire and expectation in equal proportion, we possess hope.

Hope is not a retreat for the cowardly or inadequate. Instead, it is a resilient and powerful quality of the soul, lingering on even when the rationalization argues that it is futile. Long after others have given up the search for one who is lost, a mother keeps the light burning in her heart, reacting to every step on the porch, and every knock on the door. We are Abrahams, hoping "when hope seems hopeless" (Romans 4:18).

My faith and my hope are grounded on the same foundation as was Abraham's. Faith and hope are a firm conviction of the validity of every promise of God, because God makes the visible things out of invisible things. The first is the ultimate in power, the second the ultimate in knowledge. God raised Jesus from the dead. So God can raise men from the dead. And He has promised me I will share in eternal life on a more magnificent scale than I can imagine now.

The fact is that Jesus made sense out of death by making sense out of life. By showing me how to live He taught me how to die. The last gasp of oxygen into my collapsing lungs is of no real consequence. Lifting the latch is not the important matter, but what lies beyond the door. I am convinced that ineffable joy awaits in the other room. Jesus has begotten in me a living hope. "But the God of all grace, who hath called us unto his eternal glory by Christ Jesus, after that ye have suffered a while, make you perfect, stablish, strengthen, settle you. To him be glory and dominion for ever and ever. Amen" (1 Peter 5:10, 11; KJV).

Beginning with Romans 8:18, Paul places suffering and splendor in proper perspective. Suffering is for a while; splendor is after a while. The whole created universe, now writhing in agony, is standing on tiptoe, as the original Greek means. It is looking down the long road, waiting for the spectacle of triumph when the sons of God come into their own. The people of God give meaning to the whole creation. Man was at the peak of God's creation. His fall subjected the whole domain to despair. His final victory will bring rejoicing to all. Hope is written in shining letters of gold across the face of the whole created order of things.

"For we are saved by hope: but hope that is seen is not hope: for what a man seeth, why doth he yet hope for?" (Romans 8:24; KJV). This does not mean that hope is an agent or cause of our salvation. We are not saved by hope as an operating principle. The point at issue here is that we have been saved, but there is more to come. In our flesh and blood we are not adapted for existence in a celestial realm. We have not yet shared in all to which our salvation makes us heirs. There is something for which our universe is expectant, joyfully and triumphantly expectant.

When hope becomes reality it ceases to function. The sight of the goal renders hope unnecessary. The endurance test is over. The waiting period is ended. Expectancy gives way to experience; anticipation becomes enjoyment. This is the essence of the Christian life. Tears and trials today; smiles and splendor tomorrow.

After pointing out how patient waiting for something develops within us a real sense of endurance, Paul makes a statement to strengthen the weary heart and invigorate once more those who feel they no longer are getting through to Heaven. Every day of our lives we need to meditate and ponder upon this declaration of divine grace:

"Likewise the Spirit also helpeth our infirmities: for we know not what we should pray for as we ought: but the Spirit itself maketh intercession for us with groanings which cannot be uttered. And he that searcheth the hearts knoweth what is the mind of the Spirit, because he maketh intercession for the saints according to the will of God" (Romans 8:26, 27; KJV).

Hope comes to our aid in counteracting despair and helps us to endure in spite of suffering. But we have another helper, for the Spirit comes to the aid of our weakness. He does so in many departments of life, including prayer.

We are ignorant of many things with regard to prayer. It is far easier to theorize about prayer than it is to practice praying. Often we develop stereotyped words and phrases we repeat monotonously and with little consciousness or real concern. Sometimes we cannot express the real concern. Sometimes we cannot articulate the real burdens or find words in which to couch our deepest longings. All of us have found occasions when we wanted to pray and could not really do so.

For just such emergencies God has given us the indwelling Spirit as an intercessor. We have only one Mediator, one bridge builder, the man Christ Jesus. But we can have many intercessors. Indeed, we are all to make intercession for one another (1 Timothy 2:1). And we have two divine intercessors, one dwelling in us and the other in Heaven. The Holy Spirit intercedes from within (Romans 8:26),

174

and Jesus intercedes at God's right hand (Romans 8:34).

The Spirit translates our inward inexpressible desires into prayer, taking the intangible and inarticulate groanings of the inner man and putting them in the words of heavenly language. Thus we can be sure that we are on a direct line to the throne room in glory if we are in Christ Jesus.

I have often found relief in prayer, especially when I was in deep need of forgiveness and divine understanding. The greatest consolation comes when I realize that all does not depend upon human vocabulary. The Spirit decodes my impulses and desires and transmits them in rational language. God hears and grace takes over. I do not so much need to learn how to pray, although that is important, as I need to learn how to trust.

God searches and penetrates the recesses of my being. He knows my every thought and intent. He also knows the mind of the Spirit. The communion between God and the Spirit is absolute. It is perfect. There is no faulty connection. The line is never shorted out. The Spirit makes intercession for the saints according to the will of God. He pleads for God's own people in God's own way. If nothing else prompted me to be one of the people of God, this alone would be sufficient motivation. I need to be one of the saints because I desperately need the Spirit as an intercessor.

I hold that Jesus is Lord over life. That means the whole life, all of it. I do not accept the fragmented personality that "saves Sunday out" to serve God. One does not turn the grace of God off and on like the faucet on a kitchen sink. God is interested in everything that I do. He watches me mow the lawn, trim the shrubs, and roast wieners. I can do all these to His praise and glory. Certainly He wants me to sit down with the saints at the Lord's Table, but He also wants our kitchen table to be His when my wife and I sit down together and join in thanking Him for His blessings.

The Holy Spirit is a constant companion. He does not remain at home when you go to work. He does not stay behind when you go to the stadium to watch a football game. The beautiful thing about God's whole arrangement is that He can order and arrange everything to work out for our ultimate good. Even our foolish mistakes and blunders can be made to fit into a pattern of life. Sorrow and suffering can be woven into life until they actually enhance the design instead of wrecking it.

I do not think it is by sheer chance that Paul includes in this wonderful chapter on the indwelling Spirit that thrilling statement, "We know that all things work together for good to them that love God, to them who are the called according to his purpose" (Romans 8:28; KJV). Praise His wonderful name! Let us all rejoice in God, through the Spirit who fills us and thrills us and gives us the peace that passes human understanding.